SPIRITUAL DIRECTION FOR
TODAY'S CATHOLIC:
ITS POSSIBILITIES IN THE NEW RITE

SPIRITUAL DIRECTION FOR TODAY'S CATHOLIC:
ITS POSSIBILITIES IN THE NEW RITE

A Book for the People of God:
Priests, Religious and Laity

By

Rev. Frederick Schroeder
With Rev. Craig Meyers

CATHOLIC BOOK PUBLISHING CO.
New Jersey

NIHIL OBSTAT: Donald J. Tracey
Censor Librorum

IMPRIMATUR: ✠ William L. Higi
Bishop of Lafayette-in-Indiana

ACKNOWLEDGMENTS

Grateful acknowledgment is made to the following for permission to quote from their works:

Encounter with God by Morton Kelsey, published by Bethany Fellowship, Inc., Minneapolis, Minnesota.

Religion for a New Generation by Jacob Needleman, A. K. Bierman and James A. Gould, The Macmillan Company, New York, pages 7 and 8.

The Documents of Vatican II, edited by Walter M. Abbot, S.J., America Press, New York, N.Y.

The Church in Our Day, approved by the Catholic Bishops of the U.S. at their meeting in Washington, D.C., November 1967, for publication January 21,1968.

Together in Peace (Priest's Edition) by Joseph M. Champlin, Ave Maria Press, Notre Dame, Indiana.

Andrew M. Greeley's *The Catholic Priest in the United States*, Sociological Investigations. A study conducted by: National Opinion Research Center, the University of Chicago, 6030 S. Ellis Ave., Chicago, Ill. 60637. Published and copyrighted by U.S. Catholic Conference (Publications Office).

Catholic Directory, P. J. Kennedy & Sons, New York, N.Y. © 1995.

All quotations not identified in the text are taken from *The Rite of Penance* © by International Committee on English in the Liturgy and published by Catholic Book Publishing Co., 1975.

(T-530)

PREFACE

I think especially in one-on-one situations I am quite adept at expressing myself, but I am not good at putting my beliefs in writing. I feel with my whole heart and soul that spiritual direction is an essential part of the Rite of Penance because it has had such a profound influence for good in my life. It is hard for me, however, to get my beliefs down on a page.

Therefore, I want especially to thank Rev. Craig Meyers, who with even greater insight than I had at the time, worked with me on the first edition of this book. As I have been revising the text I have been glad to find that those thoughts he helped me put in writing twenty years ago are much more relevant today.

I also want to express my gratitude to the late Howard Cavalero of the Catholic Book Publishing Company for taking a chance on the book, his son Robert, and Mike Buono without whose aid neither edition of this book would have been published, and to Claire Magna, Patricia Wright, and indirectly Alice Martin, who helped me, as she puts it, "to stay on the highway."

TABLE OF CONTENTS

INTRODUCTION

When this book was first printed in 1977, it appeared that the New Rite of Penance (the Rite Of Reconciliation) would offer a wonderful opportunity for both the priests and the people to receive the spiritual direction they so desperately need. I noted in that introduction that both the laity and the clergy face much more difficult and complex circumstances in their daily lives than they ever did before and therefore need other than simplistic answers to their problems. I was excited by the possibilities the new rite provides for meeting that spiritual hunger so evident all around us.

Unfortunately, however, now some twenty years later, the indifference of both the laity and the clergy toward confession has increased rather than lessened because, in many instances, the rite has become standardized to the point of being static ritual. For the first year or two, especially at Christmas and Easter, the form of the rite for reconciliation of several penitents with individual confession and absolution was a real success in parishes across the country. There were enough priests to give each penitent adequate time for confession and to allow them to make appointments for further help if necessary. But now in the same parish where we used to need eighteen priests to hear confessions for a couple of hours we are down to eight in less than an hour. The drop in the importance of confession to the people throughout the Church demonstrates the need for something more than immediate absolution. And the great potential is still there in the rite for real spiritual direction.

At last, as our June 1995 convocation for priests in the Lafayette diocese reveals, the Holy Spirit is breathing fresh air into the Church. Our Bishop Higi and other bishops are recognizing and preaching that we priests need spiritual direction in order that we may be spiritual directors for the people. The inability to deal with the implications of guilt, to be freed from it, can keep one from living effectively even in the sublime and holy ministry of the priesthood. No matter who we are or how we've sinned the good news is that God's love is of such magnitude that His forgiveness can free us from such debilitating guilt. Both priests and laity often need spiritual guidance, however, to help them find their way and the bishops are recognizing that need.

As I said in the previous introduction, noted theologians, exceptional priests, and cleric-academics have and are still experiencing exciting adventures of the Spirit, finding personal renewal through the process of spiritual direction. The experiences range from monastery sabbaticals, to the integration of Christianity and Eastern philosophies, to priests or people getting together to become a support group for each other. Spiritual direction, while becoming more visible, however, remains the exotic and extraordinary experience of the few.

And yet, as one reads the Scripture, the history of the early Church, and the directives of the Apostles and Fathers, it is clear that what now has such technical meaning was once the norm for all Christians. It was the task of the Apostle, Priest and Pastor, to provide spiritual food and guidance for his people. As the hierarchy developed, it was its task to direct the spiritual life of priests and people. For most of the life of the Church, a constant, regular, disciplined and conscious process of spiritual direction was both the right and the responsibility of every Christian. Something is being said in response to statistical indicators of the loss of regular Mass and confessional participation among the laity when their Christian right—an intelligent, understandable and sustaining program of spiritual guidance—is still more often seen as the exotic exception instead of the rule.

As a priest for fifty-four years, I, like many others, have experienced the ups and downs, the highs and lows of my feeling for the effectiveness in my vocation. Yet, though I have spent those years in typical parish life, I have been privileged and blessed to enjoy what in general terms could be called ongoing spiritual direction. Special people in my life, through the universities close to my parishes and friends and colleagues, have provided me with regular and disciplined ways to probe spiritual questions, to find a loving and forgiving response to my failures, and to help me discover new paths and opportunities for personal growth.

One thing I know—whenever I was being fed with spiritual nourishment, I had much more to give my parishioners in terms of compassion, understanding and guidance. The vows of ordination charge the priest with being a spiritual guide and director to the people. Because today's people are increasingly sophisticated and increasingly troubled, the direction he gives must be authentic, personal, and go beyond rubrics. The spiritual guidance demanded of the priest who would truly feed today's people is guidance that makes the sacramental life alive, personal, and life transforming. It must be compassionately administered, understandable, and person to person, as well as priest to parishioner. This book is about the spiritual care and feeding of both people and priests.

Here I deal primarily with only one of the three possibilities in the new Rite of Reconciliation—the individual act of confession and absolution. But in the freedom of face to face confrontation, in the priestly preparation suggested, in the opportunity to discuss the reasons as well as the act, the absence of time limits in the process, the mutuality of prayers, and the emphasis on changing the life as well as absolving the sinner, the components of spiritual direction in its best sense are available for the priest confident and competent enough to realize the potential of this sacrament. In the long run, as in any other therapeutic endeavor, those hours in preventive direction might become substitutes for the hours of crises—domestic, marital and personal intervention—that come from lives lived all too much in spiritual vacuums.

With this in mind, this small book focuses on some of the possibilities for genuine spiritual direction to become once more the valid expectation of all Christians, for priests to become priests, for ordination vows to have enhanced dignity, and for the Church to find sacramental wholeness. There has been too much concentration on sin and legalism, making everyone full of fear and guilt, afraid of God's wrath, and not enough concentration on the magnitude of God's mercy. No matter how enveloped we are or think we are with sin we can experience the mystery of Christ's healing power, the mystery of Grace, the mystery of rebirth, the mystery of a new opportunity to use this past behavior as a stepping stone to something better. Through spiritual direction in the Rite of Reconciliation people can find that the life cycles represented in the sacraments, which are personal and sometimes agonizing struggles—birth, confirmation, marriage, death—become matters about which their Church really cares in an intimate and personal way.

The core of the Church's life is its sacramental celebration. If that core can come personally alive for the millions of individuals who make up the Church, if they know they are heard and taken seriously as persons, the resources of love, enthusiasm, and effort that they could pour into Christ's work would be unbelievable. May God grant that those who are entrusted with the spiritual life of the Church take full advantage of the new possibilities He has placed before us in this new rite.

Fred Schroeder with Craig Meyers
November 1996.

Chapter 1

THE ONGOING SPIRITUAL DILEMMA TWENTY YEARS LATER

It seems that when this book was written in 1975-1976 we were playing with some ideas just emerging which would help us focus our vision on the golden opportunity for rejuvenation. The twenty years following, however, were a time when the clergy and laity needed and sought relief from the storms of the 60's and early 70's which demanded our stretching beyond our comfort level. In short, it came about that nothing much was done in terms of renewal in most of our churches over this period. I would be willing to wager that the few churches now that are growing and attracting people for active participation in the Mass are doing so because of the revitalization that we sought for.

Therefore, I feel quite sure not only is this book more relevant now than it was then but also the need to consider the problems it addresses is much more urgent. The limitations, frustrations, and hurts that in 1977 could be ascribed to certain segments of society are now apparent in all segments of our society. The need for spiritual wholeness and the obvious brokenness of our world are far more evident now than then. And, unfortunately, it appears to me that we as priests are much less prepared ourselves to meet those needs because we haven't met them in our own lives.

As I noted in the 1977 edition and still find true today, the Church's capacity to be an adequate spiritual mediator between the individual person and God is declining. This involves the decline in importance of regular Mass attendance for the average lay person, the disuse of regular confession by a majority of Catholics, *including priests,* and the increasing disregard for the authority of the church's rulings. It can be seen in the questions of personnel that have been so widely publicized by the exodus from the priesthood of so many ordained and competent men in recent years. It was heralded by the decline in recruitments and the increasing departures among nuns in teaching orders. It is now finding expression among the laity as traditional Catholic obligations—ritually, liturgically and participatory—are abandoned or ignored.

According to the *Official Catholic Directory*, the population of Catholics in the U.S. has increased from 47,900,000 in 1970 to 60,200,000 in 1995 (*The Indianapolis Star*, October 1, 1995, p. D4). Although we are the largest Christian denomination in the United States, Bishop William L. Higi, in his column in *The Catholic Moment* (September 17, 1995, p. 3), notes that "the alarming reality is that the second largest 'denomination' is made up of former Catholics. No wonder that Jesus wept over Jerusalem," he says, adding in relation to the rite of penance, "Most confessors feel like the legendary Maytag repairman. Calls are few and far between. Something isn't right, right?" An August 1993 Gallup Poll of Catholic Adults shows that 67% feel they can still be good Catholics without regular Mass attendance and 66% do not feel yearly confession is necessary. As far as their being satisfied with spiritual fulfillment less than half, 43%, feel very satisfied; 42% feel somewhat satisfied and 15% are dissatisfied (*The Indianapolis Star*, October 1, 1995, p. D4).

What must the Church do in order to fill the real need for its people in being the mediating link between man's anxiety, guilt, and sin, and God's loving forgiveness and expectations for His people? That is the real question—not whether we can whip the people back in line or lay on them more paralyzing guilt. I think the reason that more and more people all over the world have been avoiding the practice of confession is that too often in the past the confessional had been used as a means to control them. When they had that wonderful faith in the sacrament of forgiveness, their confession was usually weekly or monthly, but frequently the emphasis was on the fear of hell rather than the joy of forgiveness. Probably, as our Lord said we all too easily become "blind guides who strain out the gnat and swallow the camel." In fact, one of the main purposes of confession is to lift unnecessary guilt in order that we may reach some degree of wholeness ourselves *in our touch with God and others.* How can we do for contemporary man what the Church has done for its people throughout the ages? It is to this question that this book is addressed.

This book is not about the problems of the Church. It came into being because of those problems, but it is about one possible part of the answer to the problem— namely, spiritual direction—or, more precisely, spiritual direction as a possibility in the new rite of penance.

Two time worn phrases strike me to hope for the future: the first *sentire cum ecclesia* (think with the Church), and the second *sensus fidelium* (pay heed to the sense of the faithful). *The Roman Ritual's New Rite of Penance,* the English translation prepared by the International Commission on English in the Liturgy, was published in 1976 by the Catholic Book Publishing Co., New York (now Totowa, New Jersey). Everything the Sacred Congregation for Divine Worship put forth in their decree then is not only very valid today but also perhaps more relevant than in 1977. However, because of our failure as priests to grasp the opportunities offered by the new rite, especially the possibility of beginning the process of *spiritual direction* in the individual confessions, we are actually on our way to dealing a death blow to one of the most salvific opportunities in the history of the Church. I think the experience of the last twenty years confirms this.

In the beginning *sensus fidelium* came to the rescue. When the Rite was first introduced at least in our section of the country, our clergy and our people responded in an awe-inspiring way. In a special week before Christmas and another before Easter, priests driving anywhere from 10 to 40 miles, traveled from one parish to another. This enabled us to combine in the sacrament the best elements of Forms I and II—Form I: The Rite of Reconciliation of Individual Penitents (a wonderful far-reaching improvement in the old way of "going to Confession") with Form II: The Rite of Reconciliation of Several Penitents with Individual Confessions and Absolution.

It was very successful the first couple of years. People came in droves. After a twenty to twenty-five minute Liturgy of the Word: Prayer, Scripture Readings, Homily, Helps in Examination of Conscience, perhaps the Act of Contrition or the Our Father as a prayer of forgiveness as suggested in Rite II, the priests went to their assigned places in the church to hear individual confessions. In some instances we had as many as eighteen to twenty priests who heard anywhere from 500 to 700 confessions in the two to two and a half hours. Throughout the country churches experienced the same sort of enthusiastic support for the new rite. Had we continued to celebrate the rite in this manner, people might have come better prepared for the celebration of the Mass and Mass attendance *would have increased instead of decreasing.* As I hope you will see as you read on, this rite is most important not only for better attendance and participation in Mass but for one's whole life.

All too soon, however, we started taking short cuts. There's no question it was quite a workout for each priest, although, despite being overburdened, years ago a priest alone in a parish could sometimes hear confessions almost all day. Many priests were often in the confessional an hour and half or two hours before supper and an hour after on Saturdays. Some years ago during Holy Week when all the priests in town left to go to a funeral, I heard confessions practically morning, noon, and night. What a pity we not only abandoned our efforts to provide the priests and the time to make the new rite of penance meaningful, but actually, because of lack of understanding or lack of appreciation for spiritual direction, we lessened the time. Now it seems that most of the time individual confessions in the second form of the rite are so abbreviated that they become meaningless. People say that after these experiences they have the notion that whatever they might say isn't worth being heard and that there is hardly time for it anyway. Some never come back. Oh, there is usually a public announcement to the effect that if you desire more help, phone a priest for an appointment (which implies, "Call me if you need more time.") It would be interesting to know how many calls there have been in our large deanery, the most populated area in diocese, asking for appointments. One? Two? None? We have lost sight of the fact that we could at least *begin the process* of spiritual direction. If we took just a minute or two more with each individual penitent, we could ask them following their confession to come back if they needed more discussion.

The idea of advising a penitent to return later to the confessional is very valid. In the old way of "going to confession" after listening for a while a priest could say, especially if it was a busy time before Christmas or Easter, *"Please come back again."* He could at least offer the opportunity for additional help. But few priests today, for whatever reasons, feel compelled to follow such advice.

All of us grew up with the concept that the sacraments are outward signs instituted by Christ to give Grace. It is this inner reality we want. Monica K. Hellwig in her book *Sign of Reconciliation and Conversion: The Sacrament of Penance for Our Times* points out that coming to confession, reciting a list of transgressions, and being given absolution is not enough for most people. "It seems as though the ritual itself is supposed to be sign and pledge enough without any personal transformation. But people are not satisfied with this hollow sign." (Michael Glazier, Inc., Wilmington, Delaware, 1986, p. 109.) She comments later, "For some, of course, the rite for the reconciliation of individual penitents, that is, individual confession, retains its power to move them to continuing conversion. These people are not confessing because they are commanded to do so, but because for them the sign really signifies and effects what it signifies. The sacrament points to the real examination of conscience, the awareness of problems, and the absolution, but its final reality is the actual conversion by the Grace of God. They experience not only the ritual and the ritual assurances but the inner conversion also and the latter points convincingly to the forgiveness of God. This may be because they have the advantage of being able to confess within the context of spiritual direction, but this will probably always be available only to the privileged few." (p. 115).

This points up the fact that it is a much larger problem than just the old rite versus the new rite. Why do we fail to see the value of or to provide adequate time to hear confessions? Is it because we don't want to or because we feel we don't have the time? Yet, as more and more laity are taking care of the *administrivia* that used to be the burden of priests, we do have time or can make time for the really essential things our ordination prepared us for—the spiritual guidance of our people. If we priests spent more time in the confessional it would possibly save us many hours in the kinds of things we are trying to do today to get inactive and lapsed Catholics back to the fold. The best way to evangelize is thorough the confessional. What a wonderful chance there is in this new rite even in a large gathering if the need of the penitent to pursue counseling further can be set for other times that are scheduled precisely for confession.

Do we fail to provide the time to hear confessions because we don't know how under the new rite? Or is it because many priests themselves have not been exposed to good experiences of confessions, especially with spiritual direction. I have gone to confession in times past—no big items—and all I have heard is "Say three Hail Marys"—not a word of encouragement. If I asked, the response is, "Oh, Father, you know your theology as well as I do." But *nemo judex in sua causa,* (no one is a judge in his own case). Spiritual direction can and must in time be available not just "for the privileged few" but for all the clergy and the laity. We are all guilty of a lot of projection. Instead of facing our own inner lives and dealing with our darkness, our anger, we condemn and are judgmental about others. We blame our neighbors, our friends, our fellow priests, the pastor, the bishop. When we are so vehement about other's faults, we better search diligently into our own souls so we can give direction to others.

For the laity, fortunately, some people are finding spiritual guidance in small groups: Prayer groups, Bible study groups, parish retreats, Alcoholics Anonymous. Cursillo and Christ Renews His Parish not only produce good confessions, but, in many people's lives, reinstate the value of the rite. Some object these programs are too intense, but, as in a lot of things, much depends on the personnel. "What frequently happens in such groups is that by common prayer, meditation, friendship and action, a level of trust and common faith is built up in the context of which people are able to confide their unanswered questions, their anxieties, their frustrations and resentments and sufferings to one another. In a good atmosphere this leads to confessions of personal failure and sinfulness, sometimes of specific sins, either to the group or to some helpful member of the group. Under such circumstances there is often a real conversion and genuine human reconciliation mediated by the prayer and support of the group members. Such conversions are readily expressed in appropriate works of repentance because their foundations are deep and solid and they have continuing support from the group. . . . Such groups often have another dimension. Not only do they reach into the individual lives of the members in a healing and reconciling way by prayer, friendship and practical works of mercy, but they often awaken deeper levels of conscience in the community as such concerning its lifestyle and issues of social justice and public responsibility."(Hellwig, pp. 110, 111)

These groups are providing a form of spiritual direction. If such opportunities were widely available to people through the rite of penance as intended how much closer our Church would come to serving as Christ desired. The issue to which our Lord addressed Himself most frequently in the Gospel accounts was the incapacity of man to do anything constructive as long as he was constrained and inhibited by the cycle of guilt and failure that comes from living rigidly under the burden of law alone. Social scientists only reinforce the fact that our Lord addressed this crucial issue in the human personality. It is our inability to deal with the implications of our guilt, to be freed from it, redeemed from it, that keeps us from living effectively. And it is our incapacity to see beyond failures which cannot be removed or atoned for, which gives us no inspiring hope to urge us on to something better than a failure-laden past. The "good news" is that God's love is of such magnitude that His forgiveness can free us from that debilitating guilt. It has been the Church's task to make that forgiveness understandable, concrete, constructive, and renewing through the life and sacraments it institutes; and no sacrament speaks more directly to the struggle with guilt in the human soul than the sacrament of penance. If there is any place that the priest needs to be non-judgmental it is in the rite of penance. As I often tell people,

"One of my main functions in the confessional is to lift *unnecessary* guilt from people's shoulders" (with, of course, the idea of helping them see the real things they should deal with). But if this rite, as we know it, is not functional, then the entire fabric of the Church, the people of God responding gratefully to His forgiveness and promise begins to fray and tear.

Thanks be to God, in 1995 in a convocation for priests in the Lafayette diocese, four bishops pointed out the urgent need for priests to have spiritual direction *themselves* and then be able to give it. So many problems that reach alarming proportions in the lives of both clergy and laity and that in the past we have just swept under the rug could be alleviated by good spiritual guidance or perhaps prevented altogether. An ounce of prevention IS worth a pound of cure. What a breath of fresh air to hear bishops speaking optimistically and very happily about what the Holy Spirit can do for us and for others.

It seems probable that many of our younger priests are also more open to fulfilling the possibilities of the new rite. According to the *1994 Catholic Almanac* "A trend toward conservative views among the nation's youngest priests was one of the findings of a 1993 study conducted by three Catholic University of America social researchers for the National Federation of Priests' Councils. On the basis of 1186 responses from priests in 44 dioceses and 44 male religious orders or provinces, when they compared priests of 1993 with those of 1970 researchers found:

* "Priests in 1993 reported more personal satisfaction from the administering of the sacraments and presiding over the liturgy.

* "Priests in 1993 feel more akin to professional men like doctors, lawyers and educators than they did in 1970.

* "Priests in 1993 reported less personal satisfaction from the well-being that comes from living the common life with like-minded priests .

* Where only 7 percent of the 1970 priests said they were greatly troubled by unrealistic demands and expectations of lay people, by 1993 the group feeling that way had risen to 18 percent."

One can't help but believe this has a direct relationship to the problems with confession. We dare to say if some heed had been paid to what we said twenty years ago, and say more emphatically now, it might be the reverse. Doesn't it make sense that if we feel good inwardly, outward pressures are less apt to "do us in"? If both clergy and laity had the opportunity for spiritual direction, it would help them set their values straight and give them more time for what is really essential in their lives.

The possibility of *spiritual direction* is implicit throughout the accompanying instructions and descriptions that are published with the Rite of Reconciliation of Individual Penitents whether in Form I or Form II.

When we first put the Mass in English we thought that would miraculously solve all the difficulties. Instead it took a while to recognize the fact that it just pointed up our problems. It seems to me that precisely the same thing is happening in the new Rite of Reconciliation. It has again pointed up our problems. Now we need study groups on it and time spent to make it meaningful like the hours and hours that have been devoted to make the Mass meaningful. John the XXIII and Pius VI opened the opportunity for change in the sacraments. It is for us to unearth the meaning and take it more seriously so we don't miss one of the greatest opportunities for the whole Church. That sacrament which was last in being revised, the Rite of Reconciliation, may well be the first in importance. Confession needs to be rediscovered. It is the Ancient Path to Modern Spiritual Wholeness.

Chapter 2

PERSONAL AND DIOCESAN HISTORY

Spiritual direction, as it will be used in this book and as it might be applied to the new rite, centers around what the ancients called *process*. It was officially instituted in the 6th century to revive the spiritual life of monks and people, whose religious lives had fallen into disarray. The penitent came to his director, and then, in a face to face *process*, the nature of the problem, sin, or impediment was discussed and understood. Then, proper tools were provided for the penitent to overcome the problem, and forgiveness was a part of the working out of more productive ways of living. The purpose of the "process" is to understand the sin as well as seek absolution from it, and to prepare the person for a more healthy outlook and more productive life, instead of attempting to deny sin's power through sterile ritual words.

Any one of us who has truly struggled against temptation knows the power of sin. It is not enough to recite a few words and declare that sin is rendered non-existent. And with the tools and techniques available to the individual priest in today's world, he is prepared to make renewal a part of the process as well as forgiveness. If we determine to accept this new rite as one more ritual to memorize and one more obligation to fulfill, then the decline in the quality of spiritual life throughout the Church will continue. But, if we decide to enthusiastically explore all the creative possibilities in the process for individual renewal and spiritual health, then we may be emerging into a new era of greatness for the Church we all love.

The dynamics of spiritual direction as a *process* have been present in the Church since its inception. It is true that spiritual direction, by name, came into being during the sixth century because bishops and abbots realized that the increasingly stylized practices of penance, confession and absolution provided no means of redirecting the life of the penitent. Forgiveness could be affirmed, but renewal and reformation of one's moral character remained incomplete.

A *process* was initiated which involved the director and penitent in an intimate relationship. Sin was understood, not just recounted. Guilt was dealt with, not merely waved away. Forgiveness became a practical means to spiritual liberation, not just a theological assertion. The director led the penitent into an authentic confession in which the dynamics, motivations and components of one's sin were dealt with. In the end, practical alternatives, with appropriate methods and tools, were provided in order to avoid endless repetition of past error.

This process was an implicit and recognizable part of the relationship of Jesus with his disciples. It was a part of the instruction that Paul wrote to the emerging churches. And, most importantly for us, the *process* is an expectation that the laity will increasingly bring to the parish priest today as the new rite and penance is understood and accepted. Some priests and parishioners will naturally cling to the familiarity of the traditional nature of the confessional, but it is hard to imagine in our mobile and searching world a parish in which a priest will not be asked to *assume the role of spiritual director* in the coming years. Some of his people will insist that the Church's most immediate mediator will become involved in their lives on *a deeper level* of direction than ever before. And the question arises, "Are we ready to become adequate spiritual directors to our people when we have practiced so seldom and used so sparingly this tool in our own lives?" Will the opportunities provided by this new rite be an occasion for renewal and growth at every level in the Church's life, or will we, in our apprehension and insecurity, retreat in the new rite by further stylization?

It is my contention that if we priests are really honest with ourselves, we must admit that we are all more than a little apprehensive about the prospect of exposing our own inner lives to the scrutiny of a spiritual director, as well as feeling inadequate to accept and deal with the responsibility that comes with that same level of intimacy with our own parishioners. There is safety behind the barriers of ritual. There is security in having an authoritative pre-fit form for every occasion. There is risk for a priest in dealing with another human being as an individual whose problems are unique to his own circumstances and whose possibilities must be weighed on their own merit.

Therefore, it is necessary to deal with this issue on a gut level as well as an objective level. We can demonstrate irrefutably by statistics and studies that this kind of process is needed. We can refer to the spiritual state of the laity of the Church at large until we amass an overwhelming weight of evidence. But unless the parish priest sees the possibilities of the process for his own life and his ministry, unless the front line clergyman overcomes his inhibitions and anxieties, then we will indeed be talking about only another new rite and not about renewal.

Like many other priests, I have read the studies on the American priesthood, I have followed the publication of statistics, and I have observed the changes in recent years that have occurred in my own parish. These things point up my own convictions about the value and appropriateness of the new rite and the attendant possibility of instituting genuine spiritual direction into the life of the Church.

But my real interest, the bedrock motivation of my determination to pursue this new possibility, comes from my personal experience as a priest. In my fifty-four years as a parish priest, I have been fortunate to be exposed, by happenstance, to a genuine experience of spiritual direction. At times I have yearned for such guidance when it was nowhere to be found, and the quality of my ministry suffered. At still other times, when the opportunity presented itself, I avoided exposing myself to the scrutiny that such direction demanded, and struggled on more confused and frustrated. But, when I found the kind of guidance that lifted me up as an individual and enhanced my effectiveness as a priest, it has more often been outside the regularly provided channels of normal ecclesiastical experience. It is not that I searched out non-Catholics or ecclesiastical deviates, but such direction has never in recent times been a regularly structured part of our lives.

Let me explain. It is no dramatic revelation to suggest that most priests have doubts, fears, and inhibitions that affect their own emotional health and priestly effectiveness. The sins and failures of priests are nowhere nearly as exciting or interesting as most critics of the clergy would make them out to be. Most parish priests are men of honor, commitment, industry and skill. However, the magnitude of their tasks and the nature of the claims of ordination lead them into internal struggles with doubts and feelings of inadequacy that few other people will ever experience. The priest is to be an example of purity, but despite ordination he remains a human, subject to human desires and temptations. A priest is representative of God's wisdom to his people, but he most certainly has questions and doubts. The priest is entrusted with the most holy manifestations of God's presence among men, yet he knows his own unworthiness.

In all honesty, what priest among us has not had struggles with his own desires, doubts about his worthiness, apprehensiveness about his courage and faith, and questions about his beliefs? And how can he deal with these feelings? If he exposes those weaknesses to those who look to him for guidance, he often feels that his value to them will be diminished. If he goes to a superior, he often feels that he will jeopardize his vocational future. The priest goes about a demanding and draining task, expected to appear infallible, but very often feeling most fallible and vulnerable.

In recent years, the theological understanding of the human capacity for sin, especially among the clergy, has faded in the popular mentality. If sin, or the capacity to sin, is really felt, deep down, to be unnatural and revolting, then it is impossible to provide natural means of dealing with that sin. No matter how much we may openly scoff at the idea, we very often so fear the practical consequence of dealing with our weaknesses because that first demands admitting them. The history of the Church indicates that this has not always been the case. The process about which this book is concerned has, in times past, been a means of dealing with and overcoming those weaknesses we are now afraid to admit are a natural part of our lives.

In the seminary, I experienced the usual doubts about my vocation. Was my faith strong enough? Did I, deep down, really believe every doctrine I would be expected to affirm at ordination? Was I really ready to live a life devoid of my own family? Were my motivations pure? These are not unusual questions for seminarians. Unfortunately, often they are not resolved, but merely avoided until enough time passed so that we felt we are too committed to a course of action to change directions. Such questions do not go away; they crop up in new ways in new guises throughout a priest's career.

It was my good fortune to be referred to a Maria-Laach monk who served as my personal spiritual director for many years. He filled the same capacity for many people all over the world. This man was prepared by circumstance, as well as ordination and training, to be a spiritual director in a way that few priests ever are. Before World War II, he escaped Nazi Germany, being forced to leave his family and friends behind. The demands upon his personality during that time were unbelievable, and he experienced a nervous breakdown that would have been permanently disabling to many people. However, he was fortunate enough to have access to psychiatric help and painstakingly worked through his own guilt and hurt over leaving his loved ones behind and became a renewed man, spiritually and emotionally. He could bring to me the spiritual insights of a mature and committed priest, as well as the practical application of contemporary knowledge about human motivations and personality. Periodically, throughout my early years as a priest, his guidance was the decisive factor in my best efforts and provided insights that helped me attempt to fulfill my vocation with as much integrity and skill as I could muster. This kind of experience is something that should be a legitimate expectation for every priest and parishioner if it is needed and desired. It provides a medium wherein the Christian can deal with his own sin in practical, remedial terms, and no longer relegate it to a mystical realm beyond the grasp of ordinary solutions.

My spiritual director died, and grateful for his influence in my life, I continued a rather ordinary career. As long as things remained stable, I was confident that I was doing what was expected of me in a creditable way. I probably would have continued to be a relatively untroubled worker in the vineyard for the rest of my days were it not for that bombshell called Vatican II.

Like a great many American priests I had quietly railed at the Church's seeming failure to recognize that the Catholic Church was no longer a central European entity with a few dependent outposts on the frontiers of the world. I felt stifled by the inability to escape the rigid forms of the distant past and wished at the same time to be allowed in some modified way to utilize the vitality of the language, people and culture of a Church that was growing in numbers and wealth to be as vital and strong as the more ancient churches in Europe. I felt restricted in the lack of freedom to utilize new gifts and resources to enrich the life and worship of people in my parish. Privately, and safely, I complained that the Church was locked into the past. I yearned, like many others, for a fresh wind to blow through the Church and bring alive the gifts, talents, and capacities of this age in this nation. And then John XXIII announced that fresh wind. The possibilities for which I had called were now there. The freedom, the discretion, the initiative, were now mine in a way I had never experienced. And like a great many of my peers, I was literally scared to death.

In the first place, we priests were being exposed to the critical scrutiny of our people in a way that we had never been before. Those forms we had railed at, those structures we had berated, those antique ideas we had scoffed at had served to place barriers between the reality of our real natures and the perceptions of our people in a protective way. The Latin Mass, the old traditions served to make us holy, sacred, respected and revered by virtue of our office and the sacredness of our mysterious trust. Now we were told to be the ones responsible for much of our public activity as priests. In short, we were to be judged by performance and not on our ordination. That is a frightening change in stature in midcareer for even the strongest of persons.

But even more threatening to many priests was the awesome responsibility of drawing a line between the holy and eternal truths of the Church's beliefs and practices and the discretionary techniques by which those truths are exercised and presented. For the priest who truly respected and loved the Church, the questions of how far one went in making the Church's mysteries explicit before the mystery was defiled was a nagging question.

The Church, as a constantly growing and reforming institution, has always had to deal with the question of "How far?" If Adam and Eve are accepted as allegories, then what about the virgin birth, the divinity of Christ, and on and on. Once the freedom to make judgments based upon human knowledge is accepted in any area of religious life, the possibility of making an error in an essential area becomes more frightening. And, heretofore, the Church had made those judgments and the priests had only to carry them out. Now the priest had to decide what was legitimate contemporary idiom in language, music, church environment and what was flippant disregard for the dignity of the sacrament.

A great many priests harbored self-doubts and hidden guilt during this time. Sadly, there was provided no orderly way through regular channels to help priests work out these feelings. A great many priests still have only succeeded in repressing these feelings instead of dealing with them, while others, torn apart by the internal struggle, have left the Church for good.

I remember so vividly one experience during those first months following Vatican II. There was a rush to sign up for workshops and seminars on the new liturgy and other questions following the Council's first publications. There was excitement and unrest and a desire to see what the fuss was all about. I attended one conference on the liturgy led by some of the most notable scholars in this field. One evening I was fortunate enough to find myself alone in the company of several of these experts. I felt that a great possibility existed for me in this moment. These were men who had been where the action was. These were people in the forefront of renewal. They had actually participated in the studies that had led to the development of the Vatican II documents. Very tentatively, I said, "Father, I am having a crisis of faith in these new times." Their reaction devastated me. Instead of new insights or a sensitivity that evidenced the new state of the Church's renewal, these leaders in the vanguard of openness in the Church's life scolded me like so many nuns in grade school when I had been naughty.

Up to this time, we have talked a good game in terms of openness, sensitivity, spiritual renewal, and preparation to accept and use the secular as well as spiritual tools that God has set before us, but we are painfully afraid of the self-exposure required to receive spiritual guidance, and the assumption of responsibility necessary if we are to give it. Many times in my life I have enjoyed a process akin to spiritual direction outside the ordinary channels of the Church with friends of depth and insight. I have been able to give and receive in these interchanges. But until now, they have been relationships that have fortuitously occurred, not ministries provided by our Church. They occurred outside the arena of ministry, service, duty and spiritual ties in which I have chosen and been chosen to live my life. And, as such, they have been vastly inferior to the same experiences when integrated into the ongoing life of a priest, bishop, member of a religious order or lay person as he lives out his relationship with his Church.

This love-hate, push-pull relationship of priests with the various possibilities for growth in personal depth has been illustrated many times in our own Diocese of Lafayette, as I am sure it has been in every Diocese throughout the country. The Archdiocese of Chicago sent out a questionnaire to its priests asking them to list their needs in order of importance. Ten possible selections were provided. Spiritual direction was not one of the numbers provided, yet still came in at the top of the list as the greatest need of the respondents. Yet, the fact remains that the experience throughout the country has shown that, when provided an opportunity to actually risk themselves and participate in such self-explanation, an overwhelming majority of priests simply refuse to act. Fear of the unknown, fear of exposure to self and others of things we may not like about ourselves, fear of inhibiting occupational advancement, fear of being required to admit weakness, all these restrain priests and lay persons who cry out for spiritual growth from reaching out and accepting it.

For a number of years, within the Lafayette Diocese, Bishop Raymond Gallagher cooperated with various groups of priests throughout the Diocese in providing a great many possibilities for growth. Since Vatican II, the bishop, the people and the priests have realized that they are all involved in a growing process, and from time to time a cry is heard for this or that answer to the malaise and directionlessness that sometimes seems to afflict us.

We have had face to face confrontations with the bishop over different issues in retreat settings. We have had workshops led by psychologists concerning vocational adjustments. We have had any number of continuing educational opportunities from in-depth studies on issues, doctrines, liturgy, scripture, to practical matters like CCD programs.

In all of these circumstances, most of us have reached out for some answer that would give us a direction to follow, some recourse to inner security, some sense that we are moving toward a more fulfilling phase of our vocations. But when we are called upon to expose ourselves, to deal with the subject as it relates to our own weaknesses and limitations, we assume a cynical sort of sophistication. Crying out for genuine personal relationships, we become detached and flippant when we are called upon to risk initiating them. This is not true of all priests, obviously. But it is representative of a dynamic that can be observed time and time again at meetings called to meet needs expressed by priests themselves.

It is the purpose of this book to suggest that a provision for the openness we seek but fear may be before us in a way that has not been available for many decades. A spiritual answer to a spiritual question, a practical as well as a doctrinaire approach to the greatest inner needs of persons, this may be a possibility in this new rite, this new tool that the Church has placed before its servants.

We ignore it at our peril. We treat it lightly to our own detriment. We cheat ourselves as persons as well as priests if we do not utilize this new rite to its full potential.

Chapter 3

ROOTS OF CHRISTIANITY AS SPIRITUAL DIRECTION WITH JESUS AND IN THE EARLY CHURCH

At this juncture in our discussion, it is important to understand that this is not a book on spiritual direction in the sense of in-depth study. Neither is it a book about the nature and history of the sacrament of penance. Rather, it is a book about the opportunity that the new Rite of Reconciliation provides to *reintroduce* spiritual direction into the life of the Church as a legitimate expectation and opportunity for every Catholic who seeks a deeper and more fundamental level of meaning to his moral and spiritual existence.

The premise on which this thesis is based revolves around that word *reintroduce*. In recent years there has grown up an increasing hunger for spiritual direction. Fascinating reports, in almost a testimonial form, have come from seekers who have found in the midst of promising careers, the value and life changing capacity of spiritual direction. We are all familiar with such exciting experiences. But heretofore, the modern discussion of spiritual direction has implied either an exotic setting or a privileged position. Let it suffice to point out that very few priests and even fewer lay people will either have the vocational freedom or the economic resources to experience lengthy programs of self-discovery in a monastery, or in the company of a notable mystic. Further, most people will not be afforded the personal luxury of participating in a communal setting wherein the group can take advantage of an exceptional leader's guidance. Most of us will continue to live and work in places and circumstances which make such things something we merely read about instead of things we actually experience.

But if the Church rediscovers an almost forgotten fact or, at least, an easily overlooked fact that we are all sinful people, what then? Sin, in the real sense of everyday activities and attitudes, destroys our effectiveness for God and for ourselves, and sin separates us from those relationships on which our health is dependent. Where does the everyday priest or lay person find the kind of guidance that can touch his center of being and help him reorient himself? Spiritual direction is not the novel pursuit of the mystic or the prerogative of the privileged. *Spiritual direction has always been the Church's provision for all its members caught up in the basic human dilemma—our own weakness and tendency toward sin.* It could become the means wherein a therapeutic and sustaining relationship is provided between two people, whatever their station in life. How much better it would be, to repeat our emphasis, if this kind of helpful relationship could become the everyday practice instead of the exception. It would then mean that priests and penitents (priests included, one priest coming to another priest) would come to a priest acting now in his capacity and in his person as an extension of Jesus and of the Church, as one endowed by the moral authority of the professing community which is the Church. (1) Then that penitent, priest, nun, or lay person would be more apt to be made comfortable in the assurance or reassurance of his own value in God's sight; (2) he could, in time, be freed from the compulsive tendency to commit sin, and (3) best of all, the penitent could find a place where he could deal with and correct this latter circumstance.

The contention here is that the Church has always recognized this need as *the* basic human need, and it has always provided the dynamics of the process we are now calling spiritual direction for the Christian. The difference between previous ages and our own is that the Church used to provide spiritual direction as the norm for the Christian, while now we see it as the exception. The person seeking or finding spiritual direction is generally characterized as either a saint with whom we *cannot* identify, or a person who is so disturbed that he had to seek help, someone with whom we *do not wish* to identify.

In the new rite, particularly using the form for individual penance as the model, the penitent and confessor meet in such a way that a personal relationship is established. Yet, the relationship obviously takes place within the context of a worshiping and supportive parish community. Further, the privacy and intimacy of a one to one relationship is maintained. The priest, in today's educational system, has had both experience and training in understanding the theological dynamics but not nearly so well the psychological dynamics of spiritual dilemma. The process (the length of which is not prescribed) involves in-depth discussion of the problem. The desire to change is explored. The possibility of change is dealt with. Goals are set, exercises in disciplined growth could be suggested. And most of all, if the new process brings about a renewed sense of *regularity* in celebrating this sacrament, then the relationship between priest and penitent develops the potential for genuine spiritual direction in the best sense.

Again, the new rite is not spiritual direction. Spiritual direction is not administered only in a sacramental setting. But if spiritual direction is for all Christians, and if the sacraments are the means of grace through which the Church ministers to all Christians, then what better way to provide this Christian right than to use the inherent dynamics in a sacramental act? Not every celebration of the new rite will provide spiritual direction, but if the genuinely seeking penitent confronts a spiritually and methodologically competent priest, in the context of a rite wherein the above mentioned dynamics are present, the potential for spiritual direction is present. This makes a fundamental Christian right and necessity accessible once more to all Christians through the sacramental provision, instead of retaining it as an advantage for the elite.

Now the test of this premise lies in the demonstration of the presence of spiritual direction throughout the life of the Church. And as one goes about this kind of search for our heritage, it is interesting to note that in all the dramatic and exciting periods in the Church's history, those periods wherein heroic witness to faith was occurring, in which the Church was growing spiritually, spiritual direction was daily fare for the average believer.

An interesting model is the relationship of Jesus to his disciples. The Gospel accounts are more an outline of the events of the latter years of Jesus' life than an in-depth biographical account. Yet, so dramatically do events point to the character of Jesus and his disciples and the nature of their relationships that a great deal can be inferred.

The years of travel and instruction which marked the disciples' personal tenure with their Lord was obviously a preparation for their guiding the Church in its development and growth after the death of Jesus. The years on the road with Jesus constituted both their seminary training and their practical internship. They were being prepared to be the mediators of what God was telling and giving man through Christ to a world that did not know him. The dialogical process of instruction and growth, of experience and explaining that experience was very much a process of spiritual direction, because one thing remains clear. The disciples were growing sinners, not accomplished saints. The Bible is not apologetic about its characters. The disciples, even after being set apart or ordained, if you will, were still sinners. They were beginning a process of growth in the faith, but it was not a process completed by conversion.

After selection, even after some time in relationship with Christ, Peter could refuse to take seriously Jesus' assertions about his destiny. When Jesus would teach about the meaning of his crucifixion, the disciples would refuse to listen. Once, in frustration, Jesus addressed Peter with the name he uses for the tempter or evil one: "Get thee behind me, Satan." The journeys were marked by quibbles over position and status. "Who is going to be greatest in the kingdom?" "Who will sit at the Lord's right and left hands?" Pettiness, selfishness, divisiveness marked even those who were privileged to walk and live with the Lord. And even after three years with the Lord, his last night was not marked by the comforting and courageous presence of his disciples, but by betrayal, cowardice, denial. To read the whole account of the Gospels is to see a skillful, compassionate, and conscious process of spiritual direction between Jesus and his weak but growing disciples.

Jesus knew his followers. They knew him. Gently, but firmly, he pointed out the flaws in the disciples, by parable, by rhetorical question, by periods of quiet discussion. He drew out of them admissions of their own sins, and the defensiveness by which they covered their guilt.

He told them stories by which they were forced to identify their motivations with the motivations of the Pharisees, the scribes, tax collectors, and petty despots. He showed them the flaws in the fabric of their character by letting them criticize others who were committing the same sins. Then, he taught them to pray. He showed them the disciplines of self-control and reflection. He worked through their anxieties. He sent them out to practice what he had taught them, and then criticized their work. "Why were we not able to cast out this demon?" "Your faith was weak. This can only be done by prayer."

Day by day, Jesus provided spiritual direction, within an understandable framework, with a consistent process of growth taking place. The disciples grew from a group of curious and adventuresome followers half committed to a man and idea they only partially under-stood, into individuals capable of bearing the word of God to the world in the face of the most formidable ob-stacles.

The incidents of Scripture wherein Jesus confronts and heals all manner of illness or sin are only condensed outlines of what must really have happened. The Gospel of John ends with the recognition: "There are many other things that Jesus did, but if every one of them should be written, not even the world itself, I believe, would hold the books that would have to be written." The situation, the initial confrontation, the description, and the resolu-tion of events are condensed into a few brief sentences, but the magnitude of the transformation in human lives implies much more. The compassion of Christ, the obvi-ous recognition of that compassion by the person he speaks to, the total transformation, and the underlying theological implications in events of physical healing show us that something akin to the full process of spiri-tual direction must have occurred in events that have been condensed into brief and sketchy accounts.

The incident described in the first forty-two verses of the fourth chapter of John's Gospel is particularly in-structive. The Gospel account witnesses to the fact that all the events described took place over a two day pe-riod, yet, all that must have been said and done was com-pressed into one page of written narrative. Even so, let us review the skeletal account which the Scripture pro-vides.

Jesus is in Samaria, sitting at a well to drink and rest. The Samaritans, at least religiously, felt inferior to the Jews since so many of the crucial events and rituals attested to in Scripture were centered in the temple in Jerusalem, a shrine denied them when united Israel was politically divided and split into two kingdoms. The racial purity, also, of those remnants of the northern kingdom was questioned by the elitist southerners. The

Jews held the Samaritans in contempt and the Samaritans lived, it seemed, a religious life bound by their heritage in Israelite tradition and Scripture, yet never able to fully measure up to its expectations.

A Samaritan woman comes to the well and Jesus asks her to get him a drink, a request that went against all custom and expectations since Jews and Samaritans did not mix. Jesus' answer alerts the woman to the fact that he is concerned with needs greater than mere physical fulfillment of thirst. The woman, eager, yet apprehensive, reveals through engaging in word plays with Jesus that she has unmet needs, but fears that she can never fulfill them because, as a Samaritan, she does not have a sense of assurance that she is really important to God.

Jesus further draws out of her the admission that her spiritual anxiety and lack of foundation caused a moral drift. She has been married five times—a circumstance that is not countenanced by the law of Moses. So here is a woman doubly cut off from spiritual wholeness. Her sense of self is totally negative, and that has caused her to live a life that further alienates her from communion with God.

At this point, Jesus has already drawn out of the woman more of a confession of sin than she has ever made to another. She understands that she is in a moral dilemma. At this point, Jesus accepts the woman. He tells her she can worship God in truth in Samaria as well as a Jew in Jerusalem. He expects repentance. He introduces her in a new light to his Jewish disciples. He gives her a new outlook on her environment, as evidenced by the fact that she, a mere woman, in the eyes of her times, becomes the major witness to Jesus' presence among her townspeople. She is on the way to wholeness, having now a sense of belonging to God, where before she had felt only estrangement, having now a means to grow by a right to worship God as an individual, and having a new sense of belonging in her own community.

The events are sketchy. But chronologically and in their content, the events in this story contain all the dynamics, sequential order, and desired results of spiritual direction at its best. We cannot be held to arguments over appropriate time spans for genuine spiritual direction. How much time actually elapsed in the instance, or how much time constitutes a possible framework for genuine spiritual direction is not really the point. Spiritual direction is at once a dynamic that is complete in any segment of the process if genuine self-actualization takes place, and remains an unending process, the potential of which is only determined by the integrity and length of the relationship between seeker and director.

The important thing to point out is that what we are rediscovering is not a new dynamic, or even one borrowed from other traditions to be applied to Christianity. It is not an exotic process reserved for mystical initiates. Rather, it is a process that was the basis of Jesus' ongoing instructional relationship with his closest associates, and a process by which he related to all who would seek his life-changing guidance. What we so proudly have "discovered" is really the *process* by which Christians have always related to one another when they were true to their calling as disciples of Jesus Christ. These very brief Biblical glimpses are not meant to be research points to prove a thesis, but merely to illustrate a point that should be obvious. In almost every instance in which Jesus relates to people in a therapeutic way, the visible dynamics of spiritual direction are present.

Nor was the process ended with Jesus' ministry. The pastoral letters of Paul indicate the same kind of intimate, corrective understanding that Paul had with his churches. While, unlike the Gospels, the pastoral letters were originally intended as written documents, personally sent from Paul to the early Christians, the tone and content of his letters indicate that when he visited with his people personally, he directed them, discussed with them, led them in worship and prayer, and guided their gradual maturation into responsible adult faith. He deals with their needs and their sins. He analyzes those needs and helps the reader understand their nature. He demonstrates and explains the world view in which redemption and renewal can take place. Then he provides practical disciplines for living the new life.

An interesting note to Paul's ministry is provided in the first chapter of his letter to the Galatians. Paul is legitimatizing his ministry in the eyes of the church people at Galatia, in the light of the fact that he was not one of the original twelve. And in his narrative, we have an insight into his own personal development as a Christian. Most of us, focusing on his experience on the road to Damascus, characterize Paul's experience as the most dynamic example of complete and immediate conversion. And perhaps it is.

We often misunderstand, however, the difference between the process of conversion and the process of Christian growth. Conversion is a beginning. John describes it quite accurately in his Gospel as being reborn. A person starts anew, as a spiritual embryo, in a new relationship with his God, his future, his goals, his neighbors, and his understanding of the world in which he lives. Conversion is the first step in a process. As was the case with the disciples, as was the case with Paul, as is the case with every Christian, the succeeding steps in the process require continued disciplined growth in a number of areas.

The book of Acts is about the Church, not about Paul. Therefore, it speaks of Paul's work instead of Paul's biography. One would be led to believe by reading only that book that Paul was converted, and, after a few days of rest, began his ministry as a full-fledged apostle. In Galatians, Paul gives us a slightly different view. He says: "But when it pleased him, who from my mother's womb set me apart and called me by his grace, to reveal his Son in me, that I might preach him among the Gentiles, immediately, without taking counsel with flesh and blood, and without going up to Jerusalem to those who were appointed apostles before me, I retired into Arabia, and again returned to Damascus. Then, after three years. . . ."

What is implied here is that he spent three years in some kind of preparation for his ministry. As he had at the house of Ananias, he must have received instruction and guidance in his new-found faith. The fact that he uses a passive word "retire" to describe his sojourn into Arabia implies a contemplative, reflective process. It is speculative to suggest what went on during that interim, but the tone of Paul's later letters indicates that he, a person who had had the most dramatic of conversion experiences, understood the growing, guided process of Christian maturing that occurs throughout one's life after conversion. We hear him speak of feeding with milk at first, and then providing meat for Christians grown more mature. Everything in Paul, from his explanations, even dissertations on sin and its nature, through his moral teachings, through his instructions on Christian discipline within the family, the Church, the community, shows his understanding of the same *process* that Jesus used in his ministry, the *process* we call, in a more narrow form, spiritual direction.

From *The Apostolic Tradition of Hippolytus,* a third-century order of worship, we find that early initiates in the Christian faith were to undergo three years as catechumens, during which their moral habits were discussed, the instruction of the faith was continued, and participation in worship, meditation, and disciplined prayer was begun. *(The Apostolic Tradition of Hippolytus,* Cambridge Univ. Press, pp. 33-41).

What is suggested here is that every Christian, lay and clerical, began his Christian experience with something akin to a complete *process* of spiritual direction.

Then after admission to the Church, the sacramental involvement and the life in the community continued the process of monitoring and guiding the growing Christian life.

The materials from the early Church read continually in this vein. The evidence asserts that the whole Christian life of the believer of the first three centuries was an exercise in either submission to, participation in, or the administration of spiritual direction. There was no name, spiritual direction. There was, instead, the name "The Way."

Is it any wonder, since this is the basis of our faith, and the source of its power, that there is a hunger for rediscovery of this neglected dimension of Christian living? And the only way it can have a truly lasting and driving power for renewal is for it to become available as the bedrock of every Christian life, as it was for those first saints on whose courageous efforts our heritage rests.

Chapter 4

HISTORY OF UPS AND DOWNS;
OR
HOW DID WE GET FROM THERE TO HERE,
AND HOW DO WE RETURN?

If we are to discover if the Church is going to be able to introduce that dimension of personal depth that created generations of saints, martyrs, and giants in the Church of the first three centuries, a two-fold question must be answered. "How did we get from there (the universal experience of in-depth spiritual direction) to here (the point wherein spiritual direction is a novelty), and how do we get from here to the point where every Catholic has access to that dimension in his religious life today?"

This is not really a negative question, wherein we look back at a Golden Age and mourn its passing in the light of today's spiritual wasteland. Rather, it is a search for understanding of the changes that have occurred in all parts of our lives in the light of the intervening centuries. It is not a qualitative difference that we look for, but a change in circumstances that has made some forms invalid and the search for new forms necessary in order to retain the integrity of our core faith that does not change.

The experience of our times is not unlike the experience of the people between the end of the third century and the beginning of the sixth century. The radical transformation of society, political realities, and the prevailing world view took the Church from the point of a community of people who understood the nature of their static universe so well that they dealt with it from a point of moral courage and the expectation that the arena in which they would work out their religious lives was essentially unchanging, to the point that nothing was sure except God Himself—and how effectively related to that truth, in a world of capricious change and chaos, was an unknown quantity.

The conversion of Constantine and the succeeding change in the Church's status was at once the best and worst thing that could happen to the early Christian community. Obviously it meant an end to persecution. It meant that the resources of Rome, its bureaucracy, its protective armies, its networks of transportation and communication were now at the disposal of the Church in its missionary endeavors. The latter Imperial period of Rome was a time of great growth and progress in the Christian Church. Gaul, Britain, Germany, Eastern Europe were all introduced to the new faith, and the overt paganism of Rome was replaced with at least nominal conversion of most of its citizenry to Christianity.

But the price for this opportunity was the discipline and cohesion of a community in which each member knew his faith and had tested it against the temptations of apostasy in a world basically hostile to his commitment to Christ. When people were converted en-masse to Christianity, whether it was a barbarian tribe or the populace of a Roman province, individuals neither understood the depth of commitment the faith demanded, nor submitted to or sought the ongoing direction in their personal lives that prepared them to live out that commitment. Within a period of one century, the Church grew from a lean and aware nucleus of totally committed people into a huge entity in which that committed nucleus was lost in a sea of converts who were Christians, at worst for mere expediency and at best for reasons they did not clearly understand.

It was this kind of Church that faced the social and political disintegration of the Dark Ages. It was a largely unconverted and, certainly, a spiritually undisciplined Church that met the onslaught of the hordes of Goths,

Huns, and Franks that gradually dismembered Rome in the fifth and sixth centuries. The explosion in breadth of the Western Church was accomplished at the expense of its depth. And like our own age, spiritually unprepared people were called upon to face the fragmentation and confusion of a world in which old rules and standards were not universally accepted, in which old authorities were sometimes powerless, and in which the predictability of the future was completely lost.

In response to that situation, the Church returned, through monastic centers, to spiritual direction and daily discipline as the means of preserving the integrity of the faith in a once again hostile world. Man, through faith, was once more called upon to leave the uncontrollable chaos of the external world to God, while he brought order into the corner of the world over which he had control by overcoming the chaos in his own spirit. The abbots would provide, either personally or through their associates, the same steps of spiritual direction that we have previously discussed.

In the disciplined orderliness of the monastic community it was natural that the practice of spiritual direction would be written down in rules. And so much of what we call spiritual direction is modeled after the procedures that were established in the sixth century as a response to the fragmentation of the Roman world. The monasteries reinstituted the value of individual obedience and spiritual life that had been overshadowed by the brilliant period of institutional and numerical growth of the latter years of the empire.

But, as was the case in the early Church, the very success and appeal of such commitment led to the mixed blessing of overcoming the world, in a very political sense. The wilderness into which the Church marched was transformed into a superficial converted world that became, itself, the protective structure for the Church. Europe became, not the hostile wilderness which the lonely monks had penetrated, but the kingdom of God in a very specific kind of way.

In the Middle Ages, certain parts of the process of spiritual direction were ritualized. Instead of genuine repentance and self-searching, instant absolution was made the sacramental order of the day. In an age in which the Christian was mandated politically to be a believer, in which the status of his faith was protected by the state instead of being persecuted by tyrants, the process necessary to build up the personal character able to withstand attacks against the Christian life was seen as obsolete.

The process that had been the basis for every Christian life and the preparation for mature individual response to the world's challenge to the faith was substituted for, belittled, perverted, and eventually became the antique practice of typical Christians, such as monastics, mystics, and saintly clerics. The nature of a collectivist feudal society, in which all authority, political and religious, was exercised without question by an elitist few, made this an acceptable alternative to individual responsibility or piety, or if not an acceptable alternative, at least a workable one.

But we are living in a new day. Communication, education, political liberation of the individual person have made personal decision in religious matters more possible, while the rapid disintegration of old orders of authority have made it essential for emotional wholeness. We know how we got from there to here, and now we must determine how we will get once more from here to there. An individual needs to be spiritually whole as a person in today's world if he and the Church are to be more than an artifact of bygone days. The time in which it could have been presumed that someone, by virtue of ordination and sacramental magic, could be whole for him is now gone. The challenge of the day requires mature Christians, because we are living in an immature world. If the word of God incarnate in His people is to have any shaping effect on a world emerging into a new form and era, it has to be a word that is deeply imbedded in the human heart, flexible to God's changing call, and resilient enough to withstand in courageous witnesses the seductive alternatives of sophisticated cynicism or irresponsible hedonism. As did the monks in the sixth century, we are *called* to *recover* our heritage as individual Christians.

An interesting thesis is set forth in Morton Kelsey's book, *Encounter With God.* The point of determining a primitive or mature society or religion, the author suggests, is the degree of genuine freedom afforded the individual as opposed to the amount of protective security. The author compares the two kinds of religious communities:

"When man's relationship to God is therefore governed largely by social rules or invariable laws (what primitive societies call taboos), then men are given a way to relate to the nonphysical world, but at the same time they are imprisoned within the collective structure of the law which becomes oppressive and destructive. Few things are more confining to the individual and more resistant to change than a structure of law and ritual which is accepted as final and inevitable."[1]

This kind of structure is most acceptable and even becomes comfortable in a world where there is no challenge for the individual to stand up and be counted. The structure handles one's faith for him, and one is therefore obedient to the structure. But this kind of primitive faith does not prepare the individual for the real life of religious conviction. The author continues:

"Mature religion, on the other hand, comes as the relation to God is seen as personal, involving individual and personal response and reaction. God is then seen as

---

[1] Morton Kelsey, *Encounter with God* (Minneapolis, Minnesota: Bethany Fellowship, Inc.), p. 50.

interested in individuals, each unique in qualities and destiny, rather than in conforming members of the group. The importance of the individual is one of the most significant teachings of Jesus of Nazareth. In Christianity one's value is not measured alone by what he can offer to others; it exists mainly with himself. In the past it was understood that each Christian received the Holy Spirit and thus was endowed with a relationship reserved for the shaman alone in various primitive religions, or for the prophet in Old Testament religion. Indeed, in these religions, one who was given a direct relation with God was usually obliged to become a prophet or a shaman."[2]

It is certainly true that becoming a Christian, Christ's person, involves one in doing what Christ did, ministering as He did, and, in an informal sense, being a spiritual director to all who would call upon your resources of faith to ennoble their faith. We are shamans in a sense if we are Christians. We are spiritual directors if we are spiritually directed.

Now one of the reasons we have retreated to a kind of modern primitivism in our religion, wherein we allow our faith to become a collective structure instead of a living personal dynamic, is that as we have moved beyond the point of a rigidly collective society in which instant absolution made sense, we have sought our inward peace and essential identification through other means than the religious enterprise. In the last century, just as the social and political transformation from collectivism has been made in the Western world, we have perverted science and emasculated religion by transferring the quest for metaphysical and ultimate meaning from the sphere of religion to the scientific enterprise. The much publicized battle between science and religion has always been a misnomer. They are two separate disciplines that seek answers to different categories of questions.

---

[2] *Ibid.*.

The actual war has been between those who would elevate science to an omniscience it does not have, a position wherein it can answer subjective questions with objective measurements, and those who would so limit the religious enterprise wherein it is a static discipline immune to any further growth in knowledge.

Modern man, sometimes feeling that he has had to choose between these two positions, has most often opted for what is passed off as the scientific outlook, thus cutting himself off from the ancient yet open disciplines developed to help the individual answer for himself questions of ultimate meaning in his own life. In panic, the Church's response has often been to seek relevance by joining what was perceived to be the enemy. The Church's function has always been to seek and proclaim the meaning in life as it is revealed by God in Jesus Christ. Science has always been about the task of understanding the physical realm through consistently applied techniques of investigation. Proponents, ignorant of science's limitations and real value, have attempted to use those techniques to disprove religious assertions that must remain articles of faith immune from all investigative measurements dependent on finite exactitude. So often the Church, unable to prove its points by those same measurements, has sunk to idolatry, giving ultimate meaning and the power to determine ultimate meaning to finite instruments and practitioners of scientific sophistry.

The Church, in its best moments, has always used the tools of science to *practice ministry,* and the findings of science to *interpret revealed truth.* But it is in its weakest and most insecure moments that it substitutes those findings and tools for truth. Hence, a pastor is neglectful if he ignores the findings of psychiatry in his therapeutic ministry. But he abandons his function as pastor if he sees himself as a psychiatrist, or a social worker, or anything else that does not directly correspond to the central nature of his calling as a mediator of the word of God to man.

Jacob Needleman, noted philosopher and author, speaks in his book of modern man being "tortured by the times." He further states that modern religion, aware of this, has tried desperately to be relevant to the times. Then he adds:

"But how are they, how is religion, to do this? We are tortured—agreed. The scientific world-view, recently so full of hope, has left men stranded in a flood of forces and events they do not understand, far less control. Psychiatry has lost its messianic aura, and therapists themselves are among the most tormented by the times. In the social sciences, there exists a brilliant gloom of unconnected theories and shattered predictions. Biology and medicine promise revolutionary discoveries and procedures, but meanwhile we suffer and die as before; and our doctors are as frightened as we. And we cling violently to forms of life which, perhaps, were not even meaningful to us in quieter times.

"So when religion, in the name of relevance, seeks to adjust itself to the times, the question is bound to arise: is the leader being led? As church and synagogue turn to psychiatry, the scientific world-view, or social action, are they not turning toward what has failed and is failing? And has not the very failure of these non-religious enterprises shifted the common mind back to a renewed interest in the religious?

"Men turn to religion and find, to their ultimate dismay, that religion turns to them, to their sciences, their ideas of action and accomplishment, and their language."[3]

Perhaps Dr. Needleman has overstated a point. Perhaps. No one is advocating an abandonment of that level

---

[3] Jacob Needleman, A. K. Bierman and James Gould, *The New Religions* (New York: Doubleday & Co., 1970), pp. 6-21.

of truth that science reveals and explains. But we must recognize that the issues of life and death and the meaning of those two mysteries, the meaning of existence, and the discipline of personal conduct within those questions are not questions that science, in and of itself, can answer. The religious seeker can borrow data and technique from science, but the discipline or religious search remains the medium in which man continues to find individually satisfying answers.

We have become trapped in a religious primitivism as illustrated by Kelsey in *Encounter With God*. We have been brought up sharply by reality, as we tried to delude ourselves that new discoveries in the physical sciences would make religious questions less of a struggle and devoid of tension. And now, we ask again. How do we get from here to there? How do we get beyond our collectivist mentality, unsatisfying as it is, and find once more the individual bond between ultimate reality in God and our own immediate lives? How do we develop in ourselves the stuff which we can reach down and grasp in moments of crisis and challenge, the stuff of courageous martyrs and humble servants, of joyful celebrants of life in the midst of worldly misery, the hopeful heart in times of despair, the assertion of the person who knows beyond a shadow of a doubt that God loves him and will never abandon him no matter what the externals of life may appear to be saying?

People, lay and clerical, want, need, have the right to, a firm personal relationship with God. In search of that relationship with ultimate reality they have grasped at every straw in the wind both within the Church and without. From I'M okay; YOU'RE okay, to Primal Scream therapy; from Neo-Pentecostalism to Hermitis Asceticism; from Zen to Hari-Krishna, man has tried to rediscover the bond in the here and now between God and his children. In any of those areas there may be some shred of value that can help some individual on his journey toward actualization. But if we continue to affirm that there is universal truth in Christ's good news for all men, then it is not enough to provide an answer here and a technique there that gives Christians a smorgasbord of spiritual possibilities.

At some point there must be an offering of such breadth that every Church person can say, I have access to a medium that can help me draw personally closer to God, that can help me understand myself, that can help me be strong enough to confess my flaws and weakness, and that can help me find more clearly the path to obedience to my personal potential and God's universal demands. The place to start is not somewhere out there, in the exotic experience of a few, but within the rich resources of the Church, clearly affirmed and properly applied. We have access to truth. We have untapped resources. We have a clear commission and an audience that still waits to hear what is good about good news.

Now we need awareness, affirmation, orderliness, discipline, and the good sense to use the tools at hand instead of praying for another miracle.

Chapter 5

CHURCH IS (SHOULD BE) NEW VISION OF VATICAN II

To this point, we have attempted to imply, in the most broad and inclusive terms, what spiritual direction is and has been, and its integral role in the life of the Church in all times. By so doing, we hoped to demonstrate the need for this process at every level of the Church's life, including the laity. Further, we have suggested that within the sacramental context, particularly the new rite of reconciliation, the greatest opportunity for Church-wide implementation of this process is provided. Now, lest this appear to be merely a narrow preoccupation, it is important that the reader be reminded of the context that the contemporary Church provides for this concern. By looking to the documents of Vatican Council II, and some of the pastoral documents in recent years, we can readily see how this concern has shaped the statements of the whole Church.

The most important emphasis of the Church in recent years has been the attempt to rediscover and revitalize the active concept of the Church as the whole people of God. The Church never denied this reality, but there have been times in which almost total emphasis on the decision making authority of the hierarchical Church as the repository of all important wisdom and power has caused the role of the laity to be ignored. And in so doing, not only was the rightful role of the laity in co-ministry ignored, but also the responsibility of the laity to become full and mature Christians. Hence the deterioration of the sacramental responsibility of repentance, confession, and renewal from a process restoring the person's wholeness, to a ritual assurance that everything is all right, no matter what the penitent does and feels. The Church no longer accepts this implication, and is actively working to replace it with one wherein each Cath-

olic, whatever his vocational role, is seen as a full part-
ner in ministry to the world, and equally in need of the
spiritual armor of personal wholeness.

Following are excerpts from the Vatican Council II
statement on the laity:

"Christ's redemptive work, while of itself directed
toward the salvation of men, involves also the renewal of
the whole temporal order. Hence the mission of the
Church is not only to bring to men the message and
grace of Christ, but also to penetrate and perfect the
temporal sphere with the spirit of the gospel. . . .

"There are many opportunities for the laity to exercise their apostolate of making the gospel known and
men holy. The very testimony of their Christian life, and
good works done in a supernatural spirit, have the power
to draw men to belief and to God; for the Lord says,
'Even so let your light shine before men, in order that
they may see your good works and give glory to your
Father in heaven' (Mt 5:16).

"However, an apostolate of this kind does not con-
sist only in the witness of one's way of life; a true apostle
looks for opportunities to announce Christ by words addressed either to non-believers with a view to leading
them to faith, or to believers with a view to instructing
and strengthening them, and motivating them toward a
more fervent life.

"Since, in this age of ours, new problems are arising
and extremely serious errors are gaining currency which
tend to undermine the foundations of religion, the moral
order, and human society itself, this sacred Synod
earnestly exhorts laymen, each according to his natural
gifts and learning, to be more diligent in doing their part
according to the mind of the Church, to explain and de-
fend Christian principles, and to apply them rightly to
the problems of our era."[1]

---

[1] Walter Abbott, S.J., *The Documents of Vatican II* (New York, N.Y., American Press), pp. 495 and 496.

Now what is being described here is not a structure in which the laity are passively operating only as a support system for the priesthood. It is not only their money and hours in menial labor that are being sought, but their active voices in ministries of evangelism, instruction, comforting, counseling, and proclamation. The growth of CCD programs in direct reverse ratio to the decline of parochial schools staffed by the religious is an indicator of one phase of this rebirth of lay responsibility.

However, as in the situation of developing lay-run CCD programs, the emotional, practical, methodological, and academic preparation of lay leaders becomes an issue. Lay people, with excellent skills in secular pursuits of education, felt a sense of inadequacy when confronted with teaching responsibilities in matters of faith. Wasn't that a matter for the ordained? It has been a slow but rewarding process to develop leaders and teachers who feel that they have something doctrinally true and vitally urgent to teach in matters of faith. But the starting point had to be with the ordained teaching and preparing the unordained.

The vision of a Church, armed with its millions of lay people, each secure in his competence to speak for the faith, to instruct in matters of doctrine, to speak healing words of spiritual depth to the afflicted, is a vision that is overwhelming in its possibilities. It is a vision that calls to mind that Church of nineteen centuries ago that began to turn the world upside down. It is a Church of people who are spiritual leaders because they have been spiritually led.

In the pastoral statement of the American Bishops in 1967, we find the following words:

"A Catholic then has an especially critical task to perform in contemporary history. He believes that the Church has answers which no other religious community has. He values, of course, every Christian witness, every valid human experience, every man. Yet he well knows that his Christ must always be found in the holy, visible, Catholic Church. Once he has shared in the Mystery of the Church he is forever a man signed and sealed, a man with a mission. He may default his mission or turn a deaf ear to his vocation, but he knows it is there and he knows what it is. His mission is to witness to God in a special way. He is called to serve his fellowmen as a Catholic, to seek their salvation as much as his own and, in both, the glory of God. Those who have heard the call to the Catholic Church and have closed their hearts to it, forfeit their identity and deprive their contemporaries by abandoning a work God called them to accomplish in time."[2]

By statements such as these the Church has mandated spiritual renewal. Where before it might have been construed as meddling, or stepping out of his place, had a layman taken his vocation as a Christian seriously enough to dare instruct others, to get inside a grieving friend or troubled co-worker from a spiritual standpoint, now it appears that this is an obligation. The lay person is expected, according to this new stance by the Church, to be an active and direct moral witness, spiritual exponent, and agent of evangelism.

The historical place that Vatican II occupies depends upon how well we prepare and integrate the laity into the mission and ministry of the Church. All documents point toward utilizing the Church's greatest resource, its people, in every phase of life—liturgical, ministering, educational, and decision making. And the key to moving from the pre-Vatican reality to the post-Vatican vision is equipping the Church for this kind of ministry.

It means that every Catholic has a sense of personal mission. Every Catholic feels that he has access to spiritual wholeness. Every Catholic has a process by which he is led to grow in faith, personal assurance of his relationship with God, the content of our doctrinal and scrip-

---

[2] *The Church in Our Day* (Washington, D.C.: United States Catholic Conference, 1968), p. 74.

tural heritage, and understanding the inner workings of his very being as a child of God and disciple of Christ. The equipping of the laity, and perhaps, first of all, the retooling of the priesthood means finding a source of spiritual direction in our lives because we are mandated to provide it for others.

Now the lay person, on an irregular basis, may be called upon to exercise this responsibility at work, in his home, in his neighborhood and community. In order to do this, he must have an ordered understanding of the steps in a process of achieving wholeness, or opening himself to constant renewal and continuing growth.

The model must come from what he experiences within the formal Church, and most probably in the sacramental practice. The priest, therefore, needs this experience as a personal experience if he is to pass it on. Spiritual growth is not limited to academic knowledge. It cannot be mandated by higher authority or even by ordination. It is an ongoing process to which we humbly submit ourselves, if we are to have the inner knowledge necessary to pass it on to our people.

Vatican II has set before us a vision of a Church, not numbered by its ordained clerics, but by the hundreds of millions of adherents throughout the world—each a capable and dedicated part of the Church's whole ministry. The vision is potentially real. Now, the Church has set before us a sacramental possibility wherein the dynamic equipping of individuals for the mission and the spiritual growth of each person is a methodological possibility. Whether or not that vision becomes the new reality depends on whether we emasculate the new rite by formalization or trivialization out of our prior preoccupation or anxiety over something new, or whether we allow it to spring into vital new life by exercising the process inherent in its theological undergirding.

Chapter 6

STEPS OF PREPARATION

The new rite, it must be repeated, is not the process of spiritual direction which can help us know our innermost selves, root out the destructive sins of omission and commission in our lives, and prepare us for joyful and effective discipleship. The new rite is a *potential opportunity* for such spiritual guidance to occur. As long as the rite is a mechanical ritual on paper, or if it is handled in a perfunctory manner by the celebrating priest, then it only provides a written discipline for the penitent healthy enough to provide his own spiritual direction.

In order for the new rite to be translated from paper to practice, each step must be taken seriously in relationship to its potential for probing the spiritual dimensions in the confrontation between priest and penitent. These next two chapters will deal in some detail with those steps. The reader will note that they are broken, roughly, into two main categories: the steps of preparation, and the steps of actualization. The chapters have been organized in this manner to clearly show the difference between the in-depth experience of interpersonal communion necessary for true spiritual progress, and the steps necessary to establish that interpersonal relationship.

Now, in the new rite, there are five steps for completion of the sacrament, but it may well be that the most important step is the one expected to take place prior to the sacrament. Often neglected in the current style of confession, and certainly crucial to the success of the new rite, is the following instruction that precedes the ritual confrontations as described in the Rite for the Reconciliation of Individual Penitents.

"Priest and penitent should first prepare themselves by prayer to celebrate the sacrament. The priest should call upon the Holy Spirit so that he may receive enlightenment and charity. The penitent should compare his life with the example and commandments of Christ and then pray to God for the forgiveness of his sins." (*Together in Peace,* p. 175)

In his excellent book, *Together in Peace,* Father Joseph M. Champlin speaks of a workshop at a Mile-Hi Religious Education Congress at which he was lecturing. He recounts:

"A participant asked if this development in the sacrament of Penance did not imply that confessors of the future would, or should, receive specialized training to prepare for their new role. My inquirer meant the equivalent of a master's degree in counseling or several advanced courses in psychology.

"I replied that while such a formation might well prove helpful, the greatest need, in my opinion, was, is, and will be priest-confessors who are prayerful, emotionally mature, loving, faith-filled, wise and understanding.

"Upon hearing these comments, the audience broke into enthusiastic and sustained applause. The style and content of my lectures do not normally evoke such an outburst. I take that unusual reaction, then, as indicative of what penitents really look for in the priest who hears confessions." (*Together in Peace,* p. 131)

Now, in today's world, I believe that the wise and understanding priest is the one who has taken advantage of every tool that enables him to understand both the God he serves and the people he pastors. This implies some upgrading of specialized preparation for all priests in the helping disciplines, but these are not the primary qualities of the good confessor. The good confessor and sincere penitent see that the sacrament of penance is something other than a counseling session in a religious setting. Both parties must be aware that they are instruments of a power greater than their combined wisdom, and that the mystery of the Spirit's presence when "two or more" are gathered sincerely in Christ's name may enlighten either or both parties in ways they never imagined, and direct them to goals they did not anticipate. Counseling describes a circumstance and attempts to provide mechanisms and behavior patterns that enable the person to cope with his existence. Sometimes, the expectation is that if the person incorporates those coping mechanisms into daily living patterns, he may become more emotionally whole.

Spiritual growth, on the other hand, implies *becoming* a whole person by entering into a closer relationship with God, with His truth, His expectation, His loving forgiveness, and His clear promise to those who seek Him. This means eliminating destructive and sinful behavior, not only in order to cope and perhaps pursue happiness, but in order to enter into an acceptable relationship with God who gives meaning to all life.

In order to seriously move from the everyday business of our secular existence into a relationship that implies a different mindset, a different language, and different expectations from the workaday world, one must prepare himself with prayer. The penitent, through the publications and instruction of the Church, must be made aware of the importance of the preparatory role he carries if he is to take full advantage of the sacrament. Coming from a culture that glorifies winning and competitive living, he must pray for the capacity to hear obediently what he is called to be. In a world in which those who vie with us for jobs, positions, and status are always ready to count our flaws against us, we must put away our defensiveness and pray for the honest openness in our lives in which we can admit our failures, and admit the conditions we have fostered in our lives which encourage our sins. Finally, in a world which provides a multitude of foci for our lives, a thousand attractive temptations for us to pursue, a hundred models of success which we might emulate, we must pray for the wisdom to see the truth, the truth that there is one center in life, one author, source, and ultimate end to all life—that is, the awesome God whose judgment and love we will encounter in a genuine act of penance. If the penitent comes to the sacrament with this kind of preparation, he is ready for an experience which goes beyond ritual absolution, which could help him reorder his whole life, behaviorally, spiritually, and emotionally.

By the same token, most priests are captured by the secular model of efficiency and business which permeates our whole culture, including the institutional life of the Church. If he hurries from a pastoral council meeting, putting on his vestments as he goes, knowing that he must hurry through the sacrament in order to be able to speak at a Rotary club banquet, he is not prepared to even recognize the person he will encounter, much less take seriously and deal with the problems that bring him to the Church.

No, if the sacrament is to be taken seriously by the penitent, it must be taken seriously by the priest. He must *stop*, I repeat, *stop*, what he is doing, what he is thinking, what he is worrying about, and pray for guidance in the awesome responsibility he is about to assume. He must realize that a human being, a beloved child of God, who has found himself unable to be the person he wants to be, has come to the Church seeking assurance of his forgiveness by God, and an opportunity and method of reorientating his life so that he might not come to sin again. The potential in that moment! Here is a person who, if he could find the strength and practical techniques to free himself from those sins and the failures they breed, could go forth as a joyful witness to what God had done for him.

And isn't that the nature of the early Church's outreach, rejoicing Christians, eager to talk, not about doctrine, but about what God had done for them? And the priest is either the incarnational instrument through which that transformation can take place, or the mediocre functionary who sends another unchanged life on its way ... not really sure what happened, if anything, in that moment in which he is expected to meet the forgiving love of God.

Who among us can accept that responsibility and possibility without pausing, not stopping to pray for insight, patience, humility, wisdom, and courage! We must pray to drive from our minds all distractions so that we can hear, not only words, but what the person's heart is saying or crying out for. We must pray for the humility to put this encounter in God's hands, and not impose our expectations or preconceived goals on the sacramental process. We must pray for the love to really look at and listen to that other person, to care more for him than our image. And we must give thanks for the knowledge that God has given us such an opportunity to do something as significant as this. There are few vocations in all life in which a person can touch another life in a totally healing and transforming way. The priest must be prepared by prayer.

And there is one final thing that he must pray for: to find a way to eliminate our greatest enemy, the press of time. Provision is made in this rite for the extension of the process beyond one meeting. If a person goes through the process without understanding it, only to get to the last step, then he is cheated, and the life transforming possibilities of the sacrament are lost. Further, if absolution is automatic, no matter what the penitent's feelings or intentions, the whole process and the person's faith in the integrity of the Church are diminished. It is possible to see any number of situations in which the penitent reaches a new understanding of himself, his motivations, and his sins, as he proceeds with the rite. Realizing what he may actually have to do in order to truly change his life, he may not immediately be sure that he wants to give up his old way of life. To rush on to absolution as the obvious conclusion of the rite takes away his freedom to really repent. It might be necessary to send that person away to consider what he really wants to do; and then, if he truly desires repentance, a genuine change has occurred that is worthy of celebration when he returns. We must pray to be led by the Spirit in taking advantage of every healing possibility in each of the steps, instead of being controlled by the tyranny of time, structure, or mediocre expectations. Then, whatever healing has taken place, be it one iota or a life changing measure, it is authentic—and the integrity of the rite, the Church, and God's word has been maintained.

The Greeting:

"The priest should welcome the penitent with fraternal charity and, if the occasion permits, address him with friendly words. The penitent then makes the sign of the cross, saying: 'In the name of the Father, and of the Son, and of the Holy Spirit. Amen.' The priest may also make the sign of the cross with the penitent. Next, the priest briefly urges the penitent to have confidence in God. If the penitent is unknown to the priest, it is proper for him to indicate his state in life, the time of his last confession, his difficulty in leading the Christian life, and anything else which may help the confessor in exercising his ministry."

Within these brief sentences, there is an agenda that may run from three minutes to two hours. Before the busy priest protests that he could not possibly spend this much time with any one parishioner, let him realize that the utilization of this sacrament in this way may very well free many hours of priestly work in areas of home visitation, counseling, emergency phone calls, and other activities that make us so busy in the first place.

In the greeting, the welcome, the initial confrontation, certain things take place on which the rest of the process will depend. In those introductory moments, the penitent feels and comes to know whether he is being taken seriously as a person, or whether he is a faceless body with whom the busy priest is forced to deal by virtue of his office. He knows in a moment or two whether or not the priest really cares if he is there; whether or not the priest is there; whether or not the priest is able to hear what he is really saying, and whether the priest is more interested in his own image or time than the penitent's problem.

Many times priests salve their consciences by saying that their people want only the shortest possible usage of the confessional sacrament. They never ask for more. Most likely this is a sign that the priest is sending out signals which discourage any in-depth relationship. In today's world, if no one seeks out the in-depth guidance of his priest, it is seldom because he pastors an inordinately healthy parish; it is rather because they know the priest does not want to be close to them.

The priest must be flexible in this step—as in all steps of the rite. Genuine warmth may well be communicated in a moment when previous familiarity has been established. When the priest has baptized the infants of a man, married his daughter, buried his father, and enjoyed a warm pastoral relationship over a number of years, then direct and sincere greetings may take only a moment. But if you meet a parishioner with whom you have had no real familiarity, much more is needed. In order to hear what he is really concerned about, you must establish where he comes from, what language he speaks, what are the conditions under which he is living, what his expectations are of the Church, and, in turn, let him see something of you as both priest and person. If a person comes confessing that he harbors a grudge against another individual, and you do not take the time to know the history of that relationship, any therapeutic advice is mere formality. You must know something of a person's environment and background in order to know what is possible for him. Remember, the person coming to the sacrament is expressing one thing already. He believes that the Church has something to offer him in the way of forgiveness: a knowledge that he belongs in God's creation, and instruction on how to take advantage of his opportunity to live life more fully. In those first few moments, he determines whether that initial faith was only an abstract that cannot effectively touch his life, or whether or not that faith was in a Word-made-flesh, not only in Christ, but in Christ's ministry through the Church.

Reading the Word of God:

"Then the priest, or the penitent himself, may read a text of holy Scripture, or this may be done as part of the preparation for the sacrament. Through the word of God the Christian receives light to recognize his sins and is called to conversion and to confidence in God's mercy."

If this step is to have meaning, two things must be done. First, the priest must determine what the penitent's understanding is of the nature of the Scripture. Even within the guidance of our doctrinal stance on Scripture, there is a great latitude in people's understanding of its use as a guide to everyday life. To some, it is a literal law to be followed in detail. For others, it attains its effect by the interpretation of the Church. For still others, the intelligent and prayerful interpretation by the individual is the means by which it takes on authority. In using the Scripture as a guide for helping an individual understand his sin and what he can do about it, the priest must be aware of what the penitent is hearing when Scripture is read to him or by him. The proper balance of responsible judgment on sin and the great mercy of God must be selected in the chosen passages to fit the particular nature of the individual's concern and state of mind.

Secondly, the priest must be constantly preparing himself as an interpreter of Scripture. The wealth of God's wisdom as provided by His word should never be reduced to a few passages with which we feel comfortable. Also, it must be recognized that there will be times when the penitent's view of his circumstances comes out of his own reading of Scripture. He may be reacting, in identifying his own sin, to a particular passage of Scripture. The priest must be prepared to discuss all aspects of the word in an instructive, sensitive, and intelligent way.

Chapter 7

STEPS OF ACTUALIZATION

Confession of Sins and the Act of Penance:

"The penitent then confesses his sins, beginning where customary, with a form of general confession: I confess to almighty God. If necessary, the priest should help the penitent to make a complete confession; he should also encourage him to have sincere sorrow for his sins against God. Finally, the priest should offer suitable counsel to help the penitent begin a new life and, where necessary, instruct him in the duties of the Christian way of life.

"If the penitent has been the cause of harm or scandal to others, the priest should lead him to resolve that he will make appropriate restitution, if possible.

"Then the priest imposes an act of penance or satisfaction on the penitent; this should serve not only to make up for the past, but also to help him begin a new life and provide him with an antidote to weakness. As far as possible, the penance should correspond to the seriousness and nature of the sins. This act of penance may suitably take the form of prayer, self-denial, and especially service of one's neighbor and words of mercy. These will underline the fact that sin and its forgiveness bear a social aspect."

With this step, if the proper atmosphere has been established, the actualization of spiritual growth can begin. Again, time must not become a major factor in ordering this step of the rite. Every astute priest knows that if in pastoral counseling anything of significance is to take place, an extensive schedule of sessions must often be established. While there are many situations in which a direct and specific kind of confession and penance might be appropriately dealt with in a very brief time, there are also a great many that require extensive dialogue between priest and penitent.

What is sin? It is a sad fact that a great many Christians feel more guilt about things that have no ethical or moral foundation, while they feel perfectly comfortable with aspects of their life that both Christ and his Church have roundly condemned. It has not been unusual for upstanding churchmen to feel personally guilty and responsible as sinners because their sons wear long hair, while they feel a certain smugness about unethical business practices and total indifference when they exploit the people who work for them at every opportunity. In order to help a person grow spiritually, it may take considerable time to separate in his mind those things that are sins. If the purpose of spiritual growth is closer communion of the individual with God, then it is necessary for him to de-secularize his faith, to understand what are the things of God, and what are the things of the world.

Further, a great deal of work must often be done in elevating people's self-esteem by demonstrating by word as well as by our own caring. We must show them that they are worthwhile because God loves them, without minimizing the import of their sins or encouraging them to escape responsibility for those sins. So many people come to the Church with such low reservoirs of self-respect that they do not have the capacity to discipline themselves in such a way that they can overcome habits and patterns that are sinful. It is not an effort of the moment to demonstrate to that person his worth. It is a contradiction in the eyes of those who come seeking God's mercy for the priest to piously announce that God loves them beyond measure, but we do not have time for them. In their deflated state, they will almost always believe that your attitude toward them is a greater representation of truth than your words about God's love for them.

The priest must, in this step, help the person understand what he genuinely must bear responsibility for and what are unrealistic feelings of guilt. He must constantly show the person his own worth in God's sight, while he maintains the reality of one's responsibility for his own sins. In other words, he helps that penitent discover what it means to be in relationship with God, in the reality of his creation in his particular times and circumstances.

Then, real and symbolic acts must be provided to illustrate the efforts necessary in order to have a genuinely changed life. The priest must realize prescribing minimal acts of contrition is not doing a favor to the penitent. The penitent has come seeking a changed life. He genuinely wants to repent. He is not fooled into believing that some simple recitation or minimal act will have any life changing impact. To change one's life style, to break a habit of long standing requires discipline, courage, perseverance, and self-confidence. The acts of contrition must be appropriate to the nature of the sin, but they must be demanding enough to set that person on a course of living that is different from the one he brought to the sacrament. In the case of adultery, it makes little sense to have the penitent repeat formal prayers. That person must set about establishing patterns of better relations with the spouse, and severing all those conditions from his life that makes further adultery either easy, convenient, or a constant temptation.

This is an act of contrition that will help the person develop a new life. Acts that place daily demands on a person to live a better life are more appreciated than easy penances that mean nothing. If a person has been led in moments, hours, or weeks, to understand the nature of his sinful predicament, if he has been shown the consequences of his act for others and himself, if he has seen how this is an impediment to successful living, and then been given a start in practically changing that life, he has begun to develop the kind of self-understanding that allows a relationship with God to exist and grow.

The Prayer of the Penitent and
the Absolution by the Priest:

"After this, the penitent manifests his contrition and resolution to begin a new life by means of a prayer for God's pardon. It is desirable that this prayer should be based on the words of Scripture.

"Following this prayer, the priest extends his hands, or at least his right hand, over the head of the penitent and pronounces the formula of absolution in which the essential words are: 'I absolve you from your sins in the name of the Father and of the Son and of the Holy Spirit.' As he says the words, the priest makes the sign of the cross over his penitent. The form of absolution indicates that the reconciliation of the penitent comes from the mercy of the Father; it shows the connection between the reconciliation of the sinner and the paschal mystery of Christ; it stresses the role of the Holy Spirit in the forgiveness of sins; finally, it underlines the ecclesiastical aspect of the sacrament because reconciliation with God is asked for and given through the ministry of the Church."

In terms of time, it has been indicated that the greeting, the exploration of Scripture, and particularly the confession of sins, and the act of penance, might be very lengthy, even conceivably occurring over a period of months. While the penitent's prayer and the absolution may be only a few moments' duration, they are crucial steps in developing a sense that something approaching genuine spiritual growth is taking place. It is at the point of prayer and absolution that the recognition of the focus, hope, and purpose of the rite is clearly stated. The act of penance is not merely the prescription of therapeutic living habits to be maintained primarily by personal will power. It is living signs and disciplines by which one grows closer to God through discipleship.

It is in the prayer that the penitent recognizes that his ability to change his life, and the whole meaning of his life is tied up in God's love for him. In his weakness, God's strength will supplement his own. In his loneliness, God's presence is as close as a prayer. In his sense of self-condemnation, God's sacrifice of Christ for sinners stands as a symbol of his genuine worth. In prayer, the penitent focuses on the real center of his life. In absolution, the support of the Church, the acceptance of the Church, the forgiveness of the community, is added to God's forgiveness. The penitent will not go out into the world alone, seeking merely by his own strength to live a better life. He goes out with a sense that God is always with him, and that he is a part of a community of faith that stands ready to support him in his efforts.

Proclamation of Praise and Dismissal of the Penitent:

"After receiving pardon for his sins the penitent praises the mercy of God and gives him thanks in a short invocation taken from the Scripture. Then the priest tells him to go in peace.

"The penitent continues his conversion and expresses it by a life renewed according to the Gospel, and more and more steeped in the love of God, for 'love covers a multitude of sins' (1 Peter 4:8)."

This last statement about the penitent continuing his conversion, expressing it in a life renewed, is what we have been pointing toward. Spiritual direction, if the steps have been taken seriously, can have genuinely begun, can be continued. Conversion, the process of becoming a person in communion with God, can occur in this sacrament. If the sacrament is a regular part of the penitent's life, spiritual direction is a process that is not limited in this rite to only hours—or even months—but perhaps years.

And what a waste, if all the sincere efforts of priest and penitent have gone into this process for it to end with the priest glancing at his watch, and pronouncing a hurried peace. The community of the faithful are a joyful people. We do not tentatively proclaim that God loves us; we joyfully celebrate it. The content of the closing step could be simple and short, or it could be limited only by the priest's liturgical capacities and the appropriateness of the situation. But it should genuinely be filled with praise and thanksgiving. When peace is pronounced, it should be real peace: peace which God has surely promised, and peace which is within the grasp of the penitent with his new understanding and objectives in daily living. If one tiny bit of healing a person has taken place, then that is a cause for rejoicing. The dismissal is a celebration of an act completed and an act ongoing. If the sacrament has been taken seriously, both priest and penitent should be able to depart in peace, praising God for what has taken place.

Chapter 8

SETTING UP THE PROGRAM

If Vatican II and the visions that are born of its documents are to become more than opiates to pacify the rising expectations of activists within the Church, renewal must become a way of life instead of a slogan. The Church, which is a spiritual entity, must regain the integrity of its spirituality at every level, and find the appropriate means to assure spiritual guidance for all its people. The bold dream of the people of God stepping out into the world with the same effectiveness and confidence in the twentieth century as in the first is one that requires a spiritually equipped laity and clergy. The people of God, as described in the Vatican II documents, are not so much dependent on a few charismatic leaders, an infallible authority or an efficient structure as on the membership of the body of Christ being both committed and competent. This requires a return to authentic spiritual development, guidance, and living, as was the standard in past times of the Church's greatness.

To this point we have been most interested in showing the need, the possibilities, the validation and justification for spiritual direction as a priority in the Church, and the potential of the new rite as a vehicle for making provision for spiritual direction throughout the Church. In the previous chapter, we tried to show the breadth of the new rite in its every phase as being applicable to spiritual direction at the point of sacramental confrontation between priest and parishioner. The dynamics are self-evidently appropriate for the broadest possible provision of this service to the laity. To this point the focus has been on the new rite of reconciliation as the vehicle and catalyst for spiritual renewal among the laity. This is the most crucial requirement, and this is the reason that nothing less than a vehicle with sacramental access to all Catholics would suffice. Because the Church through the centuries has effectively shaped modern history with its moral guidance in areas of justice and social ethics, and because the Church has advocated so well the worth of the individual human being, the base of the Church's own power has shifted away from an elitist hierarchy (representing only educated people in the nation or community) to the millions upon millions of increasingly well-educated and articulate laity and their voices and efforts. They do not all need analysis or psychiatric therapy—they all do need access to continual guidance in spiritual growth.

But there is a big *if* in this thesis. The new rite contains the potential dynamics for spiritual direction for every Catholic *if* the celebrating priest is capable of taking advantage of this potential. If priestly adaptability in past liturgical reforms and social emphasis is instructive, then we can roughly estimate the following possibilities.

There will be a small minority of priests who, for various reasons of personality, age, outlook, and education, will under no circumstances go beyond the letter of the law in implementing the new rite. They are, and will remain, either unable or unwilling to take advantage of this new possibility. This has always been true whenever a change of any kind is injected into the life of the Church.

There will be a larger minority of priests, maybe even a third of present priests, who have had either the training and/or experience to immediately begin implementing the new rite as something more than mere ritual. They are priests whose education has included the theological and psychological background for them to grasp the possibilities in the new rite and enthusiastically put it into practice. This, in itself, is a cause for rejoicing. If the drop-off in Mass attendance, and more crucially in confessions, is any indicator of the lack of spiritual direction among the laity, then even a third of our parishes having access to this tool for renewal could be a significant and revitalizing thrust for the contemporary Church.

Yet, the majority of priests have not had either the training or personal experience to immediately adapt to the demanding possibilities of the new rite. In order for the renewing possibility to be truly a Church-wide opportunity, the preparation of this majority of priests must be considered. The magnitude of the task is of such a nature that nothing less than a long-term commitment to spiritual renewal will work. If the Church is committed to the vision of the people of God, as shown in the Vatican II documents, and is willing to pay the price in self-examination, time and resources, then there are very specific things that can be done.

The first thing that must be done is to realize that there are two possible reasons why a priest may not be able to take full advantage of the new rite. One is educational; the other is personal. I will deal with the educational possibilities first.

As the Pope is the spiritual head of the Church, and the Bishop, the spiritual head of the Diocese, so the priest is the spiritual head of the parish, but in a different way. The parishioner is dependent on the personal spiritual guidance of the priest in a way that the priest is not dependent on the bishop. This is a matter of education more than authority. The average parishioner has not had the educational background in spiritual and theological matters to converse in depth with the priest in regard to religious matters, while all priests, whatever their rank, have had some rather specialized educational preparation.

To the parishioner, theological beliefs and religious questions boil down to matters of practical living. "I am afraid of death. I am not the moral being I should be. I find that my personal existence, job, family, etc., do not match the description of a purposeful creative existence that the Church teaches. I don't feel close to God." The priest is expected to guide his parishioners in finding ways of dealing with those questions. Note that we did not say answer those questions for him, but rather guide him in finding his own answers within the confines of doctrinal integrity.

Now in order to be the translator of the good news of the Gospel into the everyday life of his parishioners, certain skills and data are required. He must know who these people are. He must know what language they speak. He must perceive some of the pressures they confront in their everyday life. He must know something about the capacity of the human mind and emotions to endure pressure, and some of the therapeutic ways of dealing with those pressures.

This implies some objective knowledge of the disciplines of sociology and psychology, not as substitutes for theological studies, but in order to understand the language and environment of those to whom the priest would communicate theological truths. There have been both historical periods and particular institutions in which priests have been educated who have not been overly concerned with these disciplines. The old days in which a priest served a small parish for decades and could not avoid absorbing such knowledge about his people have been replaced with an era of excessively large parishes with the attendant impersonality and high mobility that allows only a short time for developing intimate acquaintances.

Further, many contemporary priests have been educated in pre-Vatican II years. This means that their theological and structural understanding of the Church, as gleaned from formal training, did not include the emphasis on the crucial place of the laity that we are pointing to in this book. Further, with a lesser emphasis on lay leadership, there was less of a mandate to understand the laity. The sophisticated, educated, mobile, affluent,

American Catholic layman is not the model on which older teaching methods on personal parish guidance were based.

Finally, most priests were educated in an era in which the stability of authority, as it was perceived from both above and below, was taken for granted. You could tell people certain things in their spiritual guidance in a way that you can no longer do. The parishioner does not come seeking a cut and dried answer that generally represents truth for all people. He demands a personal answer that tells him something about the meaning of his own life.

From an educational standpoint, at least three things are required. First of all, a coherent theological foundation for the parish of our day must be built into the educational process. At the seminary and university level, an awareness of the competence of the laity must be understood. The model for parish life must include the real distribution of not only power, but also functional responsibility. The priest is now not the only person in the parish capable of performing certain tasks. The more "administrivia" can be delegated, the greater freedom the priest has to perform priestly duties. Many people can keep books, write checks, organize educational programs. But the personal priestly guidance and celebration of sacraments in a meaningful way is the sole responsibility of the priest. Even in a large parish, a staff of several priests committed to being truly spiritual leaders of their people can provide this kind of ongoing and intimate guidance. Many persons will be threatened by this possibility because they feel comfortable in an impersonal structure and task-orientated environment. But our education for the priesthood must reintroduce the clear concept that a person is ordained to be the spiritual mediator between God and man—and not for lesser tasks. Other attendant and supplementary tasks must be accomplished at every level of the Church's life, but the priority of spiritual guidance in the faith must never be lost under the accumulation of housekeeping details. A mandate to universities and seminaries to undergird all pastoral and theological education with this understanding of ordination would be a first step in preparation of the priest for his spiritual function.

Secondly, there must be a new emphasis on persons in the priest's preparation. Jesus Christ seemed always to place persons above issues or traditions. He knew the people he ministered to, what they thought, what they needed, what they believed, how they lived. Sociology and psychology are not rivals to religion or theology. They can be tools to help us implement our theological mandates more effectively. It is not enough to know only our faith; we must care enough, as did our Lord, to know the people to whom we address that faith. It is not enough to say the truth. We must say it in such a way that it can be understood. This implies a great deal more educational preparation in understanding the dynamics of contemporary life on a social and personal basis.

The third requirement is to orientate present priests through continuing education programs in these areas. Even while present seminarians are being educated more in keeping with the needs of today's Church, the present priest, with twenty, thirty, more years of active service ahead of him must be prepared to understand the interpersonal dynamics necessary to help his parishioners to a whole and healthy spiritual life.

The second area to which priestly preparation must address itself is more complex. The Church seems to be reaching the point at which it no longer feels it is demeaning to the priesthood, nor threatening to the Church's authority, to recognize that ordination does not insure a person against personal stresses, problems, doubts, or temptations. Father Eugene Kennedy in his book, *Comfort My People*, has done much to bring to light and to humanize the dilemmas involved in the priestly vocation. Priests are specially called and set apart persons, but they remain persons. Many priests will feel inadequate in face to face discussions with parishioners about certain issues precisely because those are issues with which they are personally struggling. *It is difficult, if not impossible, to give adequate spiritual direction if you are in need of the process yourself and have no access to it.* Along with educational preparation, the priest must have continuing access to personal guidance in his own spiritual growth that has neither stigma nor the requirements of unreasonable travel or time considerations.

In a questionnaire submitted to the priests of the Lafayette Diocese regarding the need for and nature of spiritual direction, one concern came back loud and clear, i.e., unless complete confidentiality could be assured, the possibility of spiritual direction for priests would not be a real option. This almost uniform concern says something very important about the present structural organization's ability to provide this service to its priests.

The suggestion has been made that the bishop, as spiritual head of the diocese and leader of the priesthood, should provide all the spiritual direction necessary for his priests. The understanding of the bishop as spiritual head of the diocese is quite a different one than that of a personal spiritual director for priests. The bishop is spiritual head of not just a conglomerate of priests, but the organic whole which the diocese represents. As such, he is accountable for and overseer of a great many functions which affect the overall spiritual health of the whole Church. Financial support, lay and clerical education, the integrity of the sacraments and the purity of the faith, congregational development, personnel— all are concerns of the bishop. This does not imply, however, that he is to be the chief fund raiser, educator, architect and celebrant for the whole area of the Church under his leadership. The spiritual gift of administration requires, as well as allows, him to delegate such responsibilities as may be advisable. This should be true in the area of spiritual direction for two very important reasons.

First, there is the practical consideration of time. If the bishop were to tie himself down to the ongoing responsibility of genuine, in-depth, spiritual direction for all his priests, even in the smaller diocese, he would be limited to this one function. Also, bishops are elevated to their position on the basis of a number of proven gifts and skills. Many excellent bishops may not find that spiritual direction is their strongest gift, as some will find that education or fund raising are not their greatest strengths. The responsible steward of the office will find appropriate specialists to function in all the important areas of Church life.

The second reason for placing the direct administration of spiritual direction for priests outside the immediate function of the bishop is the priestly concern for confidentiality. The humanity of priests and the human impact on the divine institution of the Church make certain practical considerations necessary. In a time of self-doubt, insecurity, personal crisis, or vocational anxiety, it is unrealistic to expect a human priest to expose himself to, much less seek out, the relationship necessary for spiritual direction with the one who controls his vocational future in very practical terms. Even with the advent of strong personnel boards, the input of the bishop into assignments of priests makes for a very threatening relationship between an already apprehensive priest and even the most respected and beloved bishop.

One possible way to overcome both of these difficulties, if the Church is really committed to spiritual revitalization, is to make positions available for spiritual directors within each diocese. If we can have priests assigned to non-parish positions in education, social services, and other areas of concern, why not specialists in spiritual direction? Leaders from our religious orders, universities and seminaries, individuals with special aptitude and training could be assigned to a diocese other than their own for a specified period of years. Coming from a position unconnected with the local chains of accountability could build a greater sense of confidentiality, and allow for genuine specialists to be made available in all dioceses.

Again, some broad standards for spiritual direction could be developed in the graduate schools and seminaries. Not everyone has the aptitude for professional spiritual direction; but where that aptitude and interest are found, the educational and environmental conditions to enhance it and allow it to grow could be isolated and reproduced in institutional settings. Depending on the size of the diocese, two or more persons in this capacity could give ongoing guidance to the spiritual needs of priests. As in the case of the new rite for the laity, the fact that this process would become part of a regular routine would start to remove the reluctance on the part of the clergy to seek such guidance. One receives spiritual direction as a natural part of the Christian vocation, not because there is something peculiarly wrong with him.

With an equipped priesthood, new recognition of the worth of the individual lay Catholic, and the psychologically and spiritually excellent dynamics in the new rite, the possibilities for genuine spiritual renewal in today's Church are present. The only question that remains is: How serious are we about really wanting this renewal?

There is a price to pay. Each priest must be willing to shed some of the false mystery of his person and meet his people at the point of their need. Old assumptions about the nature of the Church and ordination (comfortable assumptions) must be set aside. An expenditure of the resources of the best minds of the Church must be allocated to insure the best and most orderly implementation of this new concept. Power must be shared with the laity in ways that may threaten us. But what is the alternative?

There is no more the possibility of suppressing the ground swell of lay talent, commitment, yearning and desire for genuine involvement than one can put a cork in a volcano. The mandate of Church document and contemporary need is for a spiritually equipped Church from top to bottom. To deny this historical mandate is to deny an opportunity that comes only periodically in the history of the Church. The effective Christian is not the one who is given much, but the one who uses well what he has. Great gifts and tools are ours. The demand, the doctrinal undergirding, the secular tools, the people, and the sacramental vehicles have been provided for the Church in our nation and in our time in a unique and special way. May God grant that we use them to the fullest and that the vision of the people of God as celebrating Church, yet the servant Church, might aptly describe the Church of our day.